Dynamic Evangelism

by

Luke Tamu

New Canaan Publishing Company Inc.
New Canaan, Connecticut, USA.

10 9 8 7 6 5 4 3 2 1

ISBN 1-889658-23-5

Printed in the United States of America.

Library of Congress Cataloging-in-Publication Data

Tamu, Luke.
  Dynamic evangelism / by Luke Tamu ; edited by Julia Voelker and David Mittelstadt.
     p. cm.
  ISBN 1-889658-23-5 (pbk. : alk. paper)
  1. Evangelicalism. I. Voelker, Julia. II. Mittelstadt, David. III. Title.
  BR1640 .T36 2001
  269'.2—dc21

                                              2001003700

Dynamic Evangelism

Table of Contents

Chapter 1
The Need and the Art

The Need.

It is said that every teaching should begin by defining its terms, to avoid misconceptions. Indeed, the word *evangelism* seems to mean different things to different people. It derives from the old English word *evangel,* meaning gospel. The old English, in turn, derives ultimately from the Greek word *euangelizo,* meaning "to proclaim good news". Evangelism is thus the proclaiming of the good news of the Gospel. It is God's way of seeing that His message is proclaimed through His messengers. In this way, God uses human channels, through the agency of the Holy Spirit, to call sinners to salvation through Jesus Christ. God is raising up heralds of the Gospel, to preach by word of mouth.

We have an obligation to Christ to evangelize. Man is capable of great things, but Christ Jesus came to earth and did a work for us more immense than any of us could achieve. Because of His sacrifice, it is the responsibility of every Christian, without exception, to be a missionary in his or her own way. We are here to touch multitudes for Christ, and in this regard, the need for evangelism derives from our obligation as Christians. We must risk everything to snatch people from the flames.

The need for evangelism is demonstrated in its immense power in effecting church growth and the salvation of souls from a Godless eternity. Why are some churches growing, while others are not? An answer lies in evangelism. Churches must thrive on new conversions. A church that depends on transfer growth and not the conversion of souls is weak. Churches must learn to grow God's way, as explained in the great commission in Matthew 28:19-20: "Go therefore and make disciples of all the nations, baptizing them in the name of the Father and the Son and the Holy Spirit, teaching them to observe all that I commanded you..."

I am convinced that keys for the salvation of many souls have been entrusted to the evangelist. God ordained the Gospel to be the means of redemption. The need for evangelism is apparent from the answers to the following questions.

Are those who have not heard the gospel lost? There is no doubt Jesus taught that sinners are totally lost. Study carefully the parables of The Lost Coin, The Lost Sheep, and the Lost Son in Luke 15. All three—the coin, the sheep, and the son—were lost. All three were sought. All three were found by an owner who rejoiced greatly when they were restored. The Lord used these parables to teach about the condition of the unregenerate and the necessity of salvation. He even used His own life and its purpose to proclaim the same message: "...the Son of Man did not come to be served, but to serve, and to give His life a ransom for many." (Mark 10:45). From these examples we know that God desires all to be saved, but that without being led to God, many will not be saved. As Paul asks in Romans 10:14, "How then will they call on Him in whom they have not believed? How will they believe in Him whom they have not heard?" The answer is clear: *They can't.* If people haven't heard the gospel, it is because we who have heard it haven't gone to them and shared it with them.

It has been estimated that there are more than 5 billion people on the earth today. Some of those people have heard the Gospel and rejected it many times over. But others haven't heard it even once. In Western countries alone, there are many yet untouched by the Gospel, even those who live in so-called "Christian countries." Those counted with the untouched include the "religious" but unconverted, and those in churches which preach a social gospel or a "God is love" only gospel, but not *the* Gospel. It is alarming to discover how many nice people are so sincerely deceived and so sincerely lost, and they think they are *okay*.

I once preached in a little, rustic church in Kent, England. After my message, I was shocked at the number of people who told me that all religions are right, and that all religious people will go to heaven. This is a universalist view, held, sadly, by many. However, universalism is unscriptural. The Scriptures teach clearly that Jesus Christ is the only way to God (John 3:16, 5:24, 20:31, 14:6, Matthew 1:21, Acts 4:12, and Romans 10:9-11, to name a few). The salvation God offers is based on the death, burial, and resurrection of Jesus Christ (I Corinthians 15:1-3), and *salvation is not possible without embracing this fact.* A sinner is saved only by relying completely and by faith on the finished work of Christ on the cross (Ephesians 2:8-9). Those who do not put their faith in Christ and Him alone for their salvation, whether they have heard the Gospel and rejected it or have never heard the gospel at all, are lost. God did not spare His only Son. Neither will He spare the sinner who does not accept Jesus as his or her substitute for sin.

Will the unbelieving be condemned to hell? God offers salvation to all, and those who reject it are damned. Today especially, there is great necessity to warn people of hell. It's appalling that so many have simply decided that there is no hell. The Bible teaches with certainty that hell exists. Jesus also spoke of it, immediately after teaching about the lost sinners and the need for repentance (Luke 16:23-31). Elsewhere in the Scriptures, hell is described as a place of "darkness" where

3

there "will be weeping and gnashing of teeth" (Matthew 25:30), and a "lake that burns with fire and brimstone, which is the second death." (Revelation 21:8). The doctrine of eternal retribution is well taught in Scripture.

Currently some scholars subscribe to the annihilation theory, under which sinners are annihilated rather than going through eternal sufferings. In this theory, sinners are simply wiped out. Other scholars hold to the doctrine of eternal retribution. The latter are of the opinion that hell is a literal place, a place of weeping and gnashing of teeth, a place of continuous falling, a place where no one can die. They maintain that the condemnation is eternal (II Thessalonians 1:9). Whatever your view, the crux of the matter is that sinners will be *separated from the presence of God*. Thus in any event, correct doctrine indicates that there must be repentance of every sin, and that sinners who will not embrace God's offer of salvation will be alienated from Him throughout all eternity.

I have until now avoided answering the question whether God will consign to hell those who die without hearing the Gospel. Suffice it to say that, from the time of Adam until now, God has always brought people to a saving knowledge of Himself and, hence, to the choice to receive redemption. Those who have not heard the Gospel have always had a revealed light. Even in the absence of the Gospel, creation itself reveals God. As Paul put it in Romans 1:19-21: "…since the creation of the world His invisible attributes, His eternal power and divine nature, have been clearly seen, being understood through what has been made, so that they are without excuse." The Psalmist of Israel wrote in Psalm 19 that God's creation reveals and praises the Creator.

So there is no doubt that there is a hell. There is no question that God will punish those who do not know Him, and that the unsaved are lost and in need of a Savior. These plain truths make the necessity and reach of evangelism all the more evident. All Christians must share the Good News with as many people as possible, that more may be saved.

The Art.

The Christian's task is to engage a non-Christian into an active conversation, with the goal of leading the unbeliever into an acknowledgement of Jesus Christ as Lord and Savior. We must muster every effort to get the Gospel out by word of mouth, for "faith comes from hearing, and hearing by the word of Christ" (Romans 10:17). We must also avail ourselves of the printed word: "For the word of God is living and active and sharper than any two-edged sword, and piercing as far as the division of soul and spirit, of both joints and marrow, and able to judge the thoughts and intentions of the heart" (Hebrews 4:12). Thus, the Gospel will go forth in increased volume and increased power.

In evangelism we declare to the unconverted that they are lost and in need of a Savior; they must be made to see and feel their need. Tell them that they have sinned (Romans 3:23), that the wages of sin are death (Romans 6:23), that those who don't believe are condemned (John 3:18) (Mark 16:16), and that all must face the judgement of God (Romans 14:10, Acts 17:31, Hebrews 9:27). That is the bad news, but we must declare it! But then comes the Good News, which is the Gospel. The soul winner can joyfully point to the Scriptures proclaiming that Jesus is the Savior from sin (Matthew 1:21), that when we were yet sinners, Christ died for us (Romans 6:8), that those who believe in Christ will not be condemned (John 3:17), that those who believe receive eternal life (John 3:16), that Jesus is the only way to heaven (John 14:6), and that salvation is only possible in Jesus (Acts 4:12).

Winning souls in this way for Christ is no easy task; operating in the office of the evangelist in the five-fold ministry of Ephesians 4:11,12 is for those who have received the calling, gifting, grace, and ability. It is not for everyone (while witnessing surely is). But of all the ministries you can undertake this side of heaven, evangelism is exceedingly fulfilling! We each owe it to ourselves, to others, and to Christ, to test whether we are suited to the art, by taking a fresh look at personal evangelism. It is my prayer for you, as Paul prayed in 2 Timothy 4:5, that you will "do the work of an evangelist, fulfill[ing] your ministry."

Andrew, Simon Peter's brother, is a good example of how the Bible teaches us to be personal evangelists, starting very close to home. We are told that "He found first his own brother Simon and said to him, 'We have found the Messiah' (which translated means Christ). He brought him to Jesus..." (John 1:41-42). Another new testament evangelist, Philip, is perhaps one of the most intriguing. The account of his missions is recorded in Acts 8:1-40:

• Guided by the Spirit, he explained the Scripture to an Ethiopian eunuch, an important official in charge of the treasury of the queen of Ethiopia. Philip then told the man the good news of Jesus Christ, and the eunuch asked to be baptized right then and there.

• He proclaimed Christ in Samaria, performing "miraculous signs" and driving out evil spirits, and causing many to be baptized.

• He preached in cities and villages all the way to Caesaria. This demonstrates both the necessity of city-wide crusades and the effectiveness of itinerant evangelists.

The experiences of Andrew and Philip teach us that evangelism starts at home. After we have shared our life-giving faith with those we love, then we go out and proclaim Christ in our workplace and our community. Personal evangelism, like Andrew's, comes before city-wide revivals like Philip's. Home missions precede foreign missions. I have participated in a variety of evangelistic methods on five continents, and from my experience, personal evangelism produces the greatest fruits. Of course there are other methods and styles of evangelism you can use, and Chapter 12 will deal with that subject in more detail. It does not matter in what manner and to what extent you get involved in evangelism; all that matters is that you get involved! Allowing God to lead you, use whatever methods suit you best.

Evangelism requires constant study and improvement of skills, method, and delivery. Great evangelists, like oak trees, must grow even through wind, storm, and rain. They are undeterred, working hard to fulfill their calling. Other evangelists are born with the God-given gift of soul winning. They also must nurture this gift by prayer, devotion, and openness to the Holy Spirit. And as with any art, evangelism requires knowledge. There should be no doubt in your mind that God wants you to be wise: "Those who have insight will shine brightly like the brightness of the expanse of heaven..."(Daniel 12:3). We must seek wisdom daily, and the place to turn for this wisdom is God's Word. Gain a proper working knowledge of the Bible through regular reading and memorization. *Always* use the Scriptures. God works through His Word, and it's by that Word that we are born again; it's by that Word that we grow and live.

So study. Learn. And then evangelize, for doing is the training that makes you an expert. Do it with passion; if you're going to be effective, you have to *want*. Passion is maintained and restored through prayer and real love for God.

The grave truth is, millions of people are heading toward a Christless eternity. Therefore, it is my earnest hope that you will gain a fresh passion for the lost. In these end times, Christians must be bouyant and aggressive in evangelism. Only this will result in a global harvest and the conversion of many.

Chapter 2

What is a Soul Winner?

The fruit of the righteous is a tree of life, And he who is wise wins souls. Proverbs 11:30.

The life of Dr. David Livingstone, who opened up Africa for the gospel, is a picture of a life devoted to capturing souls for Christ. Born in a modest home in Blantyre, Scotland, Livingstone had a good education and, when a young man, qualified as a medical doctor.

He was successful. He could have become wealthy. But all his life Livingstone had been captivated by a call from God—the call to missionary work, which ultimately brought him to Africa.

When Livingstone finally organized to sail to Africa, he faced enormous risks which he could have avoided simply by staying in Scotland. But Livingstone would not ignore the call of God. He realized the value of souls, and felt the urgent need to win them for Christ.

In Africa he labored in adverse conditions, sometimes going through intense periods of suffering. In spite of this, he persevered. He kept on fulfilling his purpose. Years passed, and Livingstone carried on his expeditions in Africa despite all the difficult circumstances and ill health he encountered. Back in Europe, many thought he was dead. Finally, in 1871, H.M. Stanley, a correspondent for *The New York Herald,* found him after a difficult search. It is then that Stanley is said to have uttered those famous words: "Doctor Livingstone, I presume."

Stanley returned to England in 1872, but even then, Livingstone remained. He would not let his vision die. Eventually, that vision and Livingstone's missionary efforts opened up the entire continent. Souls were saved, schools and hospitals were established.

At last he died, on his knees, praying. His body was returned to rest in England.

Recently I flew from Amsterdam to Nairobi aboard a commercial airplane named *David Livingstone.* The whole world still remembers David Livingstone; even secular people are familiar with his name. Livingstone was a soul winner. His calling captured him, and he captured souls. He felt the call from God and followed it, though it meant displeasing his family and giving up a lucrative career.

You, too, are called to be a soul winner, in your own way. Even if you don't travel overseas as a missionary, God wants you to be a missionary in your home, in your town, to those with whom you are in contact. Make no excuses. God wants you to leave your mark, as Dr. Livingstone did.

What is a soul winner? Here are some attributes of the art of soul winning.

Military Endeavor.

The art of soul winning is most effective when those involved realize that it requires its own brand of "warfare." Winning souls has much in common with a military exercise. The greatest of all battles is not one of territory or ideology, but the battle for a man's soul.

Many who fail in their evangelistic endeavors do so because they do not recognize the need to be militant. To capture peoples' souls is a great work, a divine engagement, and it requires divine strategy. Not having a proper strategy is like going to war empty-handed. Great soul winners are great strategists. They prayerfully draw up plans, set goals, mobilize players, and prepare to "attack."

Though we must be brave and skillful, soul winning is ultimately God's battle, not ours, and our task as soldiers will be a much easier if we remember whom we serve and equip ourselves with all that God gives. It will not always be easy. As Paul wrote this piece of advice to an evangelist-in-training named Timothy: "Suffer hardship with me, as a good soldier of Christ Jesus. No soldier in active service entangles himself in the affairs of everyday life, so that he may please the one who enlisted him as a soldier." (II Timothy 2:3-4). Note that soul winners are called to *suffer* hardship, not to *evade* it. As soldiers, we will face all conditions, good and bad. The greatness of our cause drives us.

Some churches teach "spiritual warfare." Other churches believe spiritual warfare should neither be taught nor practiced in church. No matter what your view about spiritual warfare, to win a soul demands the tact, skill, bravery, and endurance of a soldier. Though the task of a soldier in God's army is a weighty one, we can take great comfort and courage in the fact that Jesus, the Captain of the Hosts, has gone before us.

Occupational Endeavor.

In addition to a military exercise, soul winning is also an occupational commitment. This is an occupation for every Christian. God has called us to soul winning. We are accountable to God; we labor for God. God watches over us. He is the one who will reward us, in this life and the next. Let us be true and faithful.

"The hard-working farmer ought to be the first to receive his share of the crops" (II Timothy 2:6). To take a soul implies a farmer. The farmer must face all kinds of risks and work hard: He must plow the fallow ground, dig, sow the seed, anticipate rain and weather, weed, and wait patiently for the harvest. Then it lies in God's hands, as Paul explained in I Corinthians 3:7-9: "...neither the one who plants nor the one who waters is anything, but God who causes the growth. Now he who plants and he who waters are one; but each will receive his own reward according to his own labor. For we are God's fellow workers; you are God's field, God's building." The same idea, of working diligently while leaving the results in God's hands, applies to the taking of souls.

Now is the time to plant the seeds of the Gospel in people's hearts, for soon will come the harvest. If you are wise, gather souls for the Kingdom now; if you are wise, work hard now.

Commitment to Love.

Soul winning is also a commitment to love. "I already know how to love," you say. But this is unique; this is the love of Christ reaching through us. The soul winner must demonstrate this love to those to whom he is reaching out. They may seem as hard as flint. They may curse you. They may rebel. But love will win them.

This love isn't optional. Jesus said in John 13:34-35, "A new commandment I give to you, that you love one another, even as I have loved you, that you also love one another. By this all men will know that you are My disciples, if you have love for one another." Our Savior has given us a command. Not to "love" with the hearts-and-flowers kind of sentiment so often mistaken for love, but to love others as He loved us. This love is an *action*, and it will bowl people over. Love wins. Love never fails.

Why has God entrusted to us so glorious a message? Surely angels could proclaim it better and more gloriously. Seraphim and cherubim who see His glory could also proclaim it better than we. But angels, seraphim and cherubim never experienced salvation—we have. If you know the saving grace of God, you will want to share it with all. You won't keep quiet. You'll shout from the rooftops!

11

Zeal.

A soul winner must be a zealot. Psalm 69:9 says, "zeal for Your house has consumed me." Our Lord was also a "zealot," always about His Father's business, even when it displeased others to the extreme. Zeal must drive us too! Evangelism is *our* business. As John Wesley declared, "It is my business here below to declare behold the lamb."

Zeal is the wheel that turns all the activities in Christian life. It's the powerful current that propels. If we allow ourselves to become preoccupied with life and things of this world, we may lose our zeal. God will restore it. When the prophet Isaiah cried out, "Woe is me, for I am ruined! Because I am a man of unclean lips, and I live among a people of unclean lips" (Isaiah 6:5), he was instantly touched with coal from the altar, which took away his guilt. Then he joyfully cried to the Lord, "Here am I. Send me!" In prayer ask God to touch you, that we, like Isaiah, will be ready and able to do His bidding. Get zeal. Get going. Be fervent in spirit.

Fire.

"I baptize you with water for repentance, but He who is coming after me is mightier than I, and I am not fit to remove His sandals; He will baptize you with the Holy Spirit and fire. His winnowing fork is in His hand, and He will thoroughly clear His threshing floor; and He will gather His wheat into the barn, but He will burn up the chaff with unquenchable fire." Matthew 3:11-12. These are the words of John the Baptist, speaking, of course, about Jesus. Having the Lord come at us with a winnowing fork is not an altogether comforting thought, but this fire is a necessary part of the Christian life. You need the fire of the Spirit. Yes, it is painful. When you go through the furnace, you will cry out as you feel your sins stripped away. But when you come out, you will be shining, clean and pure, refined.

When you have passed through the fire you will never be

the same again. You won't shut up! This is what caused the Apostle Paul to preach in the Philippian jail until the earth shook, the doors flew wide open, and the jailer and all his household were converted. It was the fire that filled Peter on the day of Pentecost. It completely transformed him. Prior to Pentecost, Peter had not always been bold in proclaiming Christ; sometimes he was downright timid. But when the Spirit came upon him, his nature changed. He became fervent, fearless. Fired up with the Holy Spirit, he faced that huge crowd and preached a great evangelistic sermon; 3,000 people were saved that day.

We need the Holy Spirit for the work of disciple-making; the Holy Spirit comes to ignite fire in us. Many churches must have neglected these foundational teachings of baptism with the Holy Spirit and fire, but we must continue to preach the Baptism in the Holy Spirit.

All great evangelists have been fired up. You and I, too, can overcome our fears and timidity and get the fire. Ask God to fill you with His Holy Spirit again. Though theology is important, our theological stands do not matter when it comes to receiving the fire of the Holy Spirit. Our doctrinal backgrounds do not matter, nor do denominational affiliations. We all agree that we are in need of the Holy Spirit, Who will make the word of God on our lips like fire, and will enable us to speak with tongues as of fire.

How can you get this fire? Dwell in His presence. Spend time with Him. As we gaze on His glory, we display His glory. It was when Moses spent 40 days and 40 nights alone on the mount with God that he displayed God's splendor; his face shone so brightly that people could not look on his face. Be on fire for God.

Chapter 3

Preparing Yourself

Both the message and the messenger are important in effective evangelism. Experience has proven that people look to the messenger as much as they look to the message. The soul winner will be judged by knowledge of the Word of God; character; prayer life; courage; perseverance; openness to change; and willingness to learn.

The Word Of God.

Every soul winner must be a keen and diligent student of the Bible, for the evangelist's most useful tool is the Word of God. Study the Bible daily, devotedly, and systematically. The Holy Spirit of God works through the Word to convict the sinner, so being without good Bible knowledge is like going to war without weapons. Memorize the Scriptures. Meditate upon them. Allow God to change you through them. Spiritual life and growth are in the Word of God, so those who are not good students of the Word are not growing, and the Christian who is not growing cannot be an effective evangelist.

Do not study the Bible hit and run. If you do, you will run and not hit. That's not to say you can't read on the run and gain—infrequent reading is better than none. But it is necessary to gain a working knowledge of the Scriptures. Those who neglect the Scriptures will be inept at the art of soul winning, and their own spiritual lives will suffer.

So read the Word. Live it. Quote from it as Jesus did.

14

Use it when you deal with sinners. In the Word of God, Paradise is opened and the gates of hell defeated. It is like a fire that burns, a hammer that hits and breaks, a plow through the hardened soil of our hearts. It is the word of truth, the salvation of everyone who believes; sharper than a double-edged sword, it pierces the heart (II Timothy 2:15, Romans 1:16, Hebrews 4:12).

The soul winner will have a firm belief that the Scriptures are given by divine inspiration, that it is the final authority for the believer in faith and practice, and that the cause is infallible (2 Timothy 3:16). Above all, the messenger must believe the message and in the One who sent them.

Character.

The art and practice of soul winning requires people of exceptional lifestyle, because our character, who and what we really are, is often looked upon as more important than words.

Sometimes character negatively distorts the message. Saying all the right words and witnessing for Christ while at the same time living in carnality will lead people to ask, "Are you *sure* you're saved?" Professing faith in Christ and living like the devil will be a major hindrance to soul winning.

But good character can be a powerful witness. Someone once said, "The sermon that influenced me most was the good life of a Christian who let me see God in him." Effective evangelism is when the people who know us are led to ask, "What do you have that I don't have?" I am not suggesting that soul winners are angels. But they should be, to borrow C. S. Lewis' terminology, "little Christs."

So develop good character. How? Read the Bible faithfully. If we neglect the Word, we neglect change of character to Christ-likeness. Just as if you don't look into the mirror, you forget what you look like, so if you don't look into the Word you forget who you really are. Also, form friendships with other Christians. "Iron sharpens iron," says Proverbs 27:17, "so one man sharpens another." Or as the old saying goes, "Show me a man with his friends and I will show you what type of a man he is." Friends of faith will keep each other faithful.

Since soul winning is a lifestyle, we should be careful in all that we do and say; in where we go, what we read, what we watch. The words of our lips should match the actions of our life. Remember that we are Christians, and as we share His name, may we share His character.

Prayer Life.

Successful evangelism depends greatly on prayer. Jesus loved prayer. He prayed always. He prayed at his Baptism. He prayed before calling his disciples. He prayed during the forty days spent in the wilderness. He prayed when the seventy returned with joy. He prayed for Peter when Satan desired to sift him like wheat. He certainly prayed at Lazarus' grave. He prayed in the Garden of Gethsemane as He bore our sins and sorrows that night. He prayed from the cross. If Jesus prayed, shouldn't you?

A prayerless Christian is a lifeless Christian. I have been in ministry for a while, and I have noted that most Christians are not praying as they should. Many even in ministry are not praying as they ought to. I once read, "Satan attempts to keep us from praying, because he knows that one minute of prayer can destroy what he has planted in many years." We know that prayer changes things: "The effective prayer of a righteous man can accomplish much" (James 5:16). Prayer is powerful. A person of prayer will change things. Prayers of faith will move mountains. Nothing is impossible for those who pray in faith.

Courage.

Courage means to speak the Word powerfully and without fear. You can be a person of the Word, a person of good character, and a person of prayer—but if you lack courage, you won't be an effective soul winner.

People of courage have not necessarily been courageous throughout their entire lives. Everyone has fears; therefore, everyone is in need of courage. Through the power of the Holy Spirit, God gives us the courage to accomplish what He wants.

One of the greatest hindrances to evangelism and missions today is lack of courage. It takes courage to talk to people about God. Most Christians are timid, and this timidity holds them back from sharing the Gospel. We must overcome it. Don't allow yourself to be held back by fear. Refuse to be reserved! Quit being quiet! Be red hot! God will be with you wherever you go. He will guide you to the right people and give you the words to speak to them.

It was this courage that filled one servant of the Lord, who stood up in a restaurant that was full, and shouted loudly, "All you people listen to me! You are eating your food like animals! You haven't even prayed!" There was dead silence. Then he prayed for the food, his own and everyone else's. Then he sat down and ate his food. The results were amazing. People in that restaurant went to him and asked him about the way to salvation and life. (I am not suggesting that we all use this aggressive method of evangelism, but this was what the Lord led this particular man to do.)

Using myself as an example, I have decided to be very bold. I preach everywhere. When I preached once in a mosque, my subject was the death, burial, and resurrection of Jesus Christ. Needless to say, I have never been invited back—but I was bold that day. The anointing came on me until I stood on the top of the table. In one town in Northern Kenya, I preached on hell in a Muslim school! When I made an altar call, no one came forth. But during the night, every member of that class came one by one, and we led them to the Lord. I have preached on the train in Sweden; it was great fun. In the past ten years I have preached fourteen times on airplanes. I have preached on a bus in Kenya. Fifty-two people were born again on that bus. I have had many opportunities to speak to people on a one-on-one basis, and as I take a good look over the past three years, thousands of people have been saved. I speak about Jesus Christ to all who sit next to me on the bus, in airplanes, in airport lounges, in stations; wherever I happen to be.

How can you get this courage to speak for the Lord? Ask Him in prayer to give it to you. That is exactly what the early Christians did when they prayed in Acts 4:29-30: "grant that Your bond-servants may speak Your word with all confidence, while You extend Your hand to heal, and signs and wonders take place through the name of Your holy servant Jesus."

Perseverance.

A fable tells of two frogs that fell into a large can of milk. One of them was named Pessimist. He said, "What is the use of going on kicking? I will drown sooner or later, so I might as well give up now." In despair, he sank to the bottom of the can and was drowned immediately. The other frog was named Optimist. He said, "I'll just keep swimming around." He kept on swimming. He kept on kicking. The next morning when the can was opened, there he was—sitting on a pad of butter.

That second frog had made the right use of adversity. He did not give up. He had perseverance! Perseverance is what enables you to keep going in spite of pressures and problems; it is the God-given ability to cope with the obstacles, difficulties, testings and trials of life in a way that glorifies God. If you have faith without perseverance, you will shake when the storms of life hit you. Perseverance is the anchor that keeps the soul steadfast when difficult circumstances come.

One who has no perseverance will be easily discouraged. In my travels I have met many discouraged Christians. They brood over their past and are unhappy with the present. This discouragement leads to depression. Psychologists, counselors and pastors spend their time trying to patch up these people, but all many of them need is perseverance.

What produces perseverance? The ingredients to it are some of the fruits of the Holy Spirit listed in Galatians 5:22: patience, faithfulness, and self-control. Like any fruit, perseverance must be cultivated. This takes time. In the midst of adverse circumstances, allow the Holy Spirit to control you and cultivate perseverance. Nurture it! Soul winning is a commitment of a lifetime. Never, never give up.

There's actually no reason for a child of God to be discouraged. Jesus had His share of troubles, but He refused to be discouraged. We too can refuse to be discouraged. Don't brood; don't look to your circumstances—look to Jesus. Hang on to God's promises. Don't let the enemy rob you. The Bible instructs us on this: "Rejoice always; pray without ceasing; in everything give thanks; for this is God's will for you in Christ Jesus" (1 Thessalonians 5:16-18). There will be many struggles, but there will also be many victories.

It's sad but true that I have seen churches that once blossomed close down. One European church I preached in was an example of this. It was a great church, but when economic problems hit, everybody left. It simply shut down. I am talking of a church that had more than 300 people! If they had learned the lesson of perseverance, they could have been one of the largest churches in Europe today. When others pick up their toys and go home, then pick up your tools and go to work, come what may!

"I endure all things," the Apostle Paul wrote to Timothy (II Timothy 2:10). Paul did indeed face many hardships. He could have given up, but instead he persevered. He did not lose heart. Like Paul, an effective soul winner doesn't lose heart. Crises are not meant to crush you. They *make* you. God turns our losses into gains, our sorrows into joys, and our fears into faith.

Willingness To Change.

To be effective in soul winning, one must be open to change. Everything is changing fast. We've gone from slow foods to fast foods, typewriters to laptops, black & white T.V. to HDTV, manual cars to automatics. Technology is changing, science is changing, people are thinking differently. Even theology is being interpreted and explained in different cultural perspectives. Those of us in evangelism see great opportunities in these changing times. New changes in life may demand new changes in evangelism.

"But we've always done it this way!" Some churches always do things just like they've always done before. You may notice that they're often just getting the same result that they've always had before, too—nothing. Something that worked a few years ago may not work today; some of the old methods and styles of evangelism will have to give way to new ones. When I was growing up as an evangelist, the rule was the longer you preached, the greater the anointing, and so I usually preached for three hours, or six, sometimes even eight. The people were spell-bound and nobody moved. If I did that today (without God's special direction to do so), everybody would go home! There's a season for everything. If you're not getting the desired results, it could well be that God wants you to change.

I will vehemently stress the two things that will never change:

God's Word: The Word of God will never change. We are not to compromise on this. It is the standard text for evangelism and missions, and the doctrines it teaches are to be upheld unswervingly. Jesus said, "For truly I say to you, until heaven and earth pass away, not the smallest letter or stroke shall pass from the Law until all is accomplished" (Matthew 5:18).

Jesus Christ, our Savior: "Jesus Christ is the same yesterday and today and forever" (Hebrews 13:8). The uniqueness of our Christian faith lies in the uniqueness of our Lord and Savior Jesus Christ. He is the central theme of the evangel, and salvation is hinged on His death, burial, and resurrection— no one and nothing else. All else may change, but not Jesus; that is why we preach "Jesus Christ, and Him crucified" (1 Corinthians 2:2).

Times are changing, and the innovative soul winner will need to take advantage of the changes while also holding to the age-old truths. The important question in these times is, "What does God want me to do, and how does He want me to go about it?" It is important that you be yourself. God made you as you are; don't try to be anyone or anything else. Look to God for your inspiration, through prayer and reading your Bible.

Willingness To Learn.

A soul winner learns by spending time with the Savior, and from accepting the teachings of those in authority over us in the church.

However important evangelism is, the first responsibility of the Christian is not soul winning—it is to be with Jesus. "If you abide in Me, and My words abide in you, ask whatever you wish, and it will be done for you" (John 15:7). Jesus used the word "abide" (also translated as "remain") several times in John 15. Fruitfulness and effectiveness is for those abiding in Christ. Jesus himself teaches those who abide in Him; it is from He Who is the vine that they draw all their strength, energy, supplies, resources, life, and everything needful. Evangelism fails when we attempt it on our own. We need to live in unbroken fellowship with Christ. Because

He is the vine and we are the branches, we draw our life, our sap, from Him. When our fellowship with Him is broken (through sin, prayerlessness, neglect of the Word, neglect of fellowship), we wither and are unproductive. Those who are not bearing fruit are not abiding in Christ and may suffer the consequences of being cut off. God is glorified when we produce fruit.

Are you dwelling in Him? Living in Him literally as you live in your home? Spend time in the presence of Jesus. Hear Him speak to you; let Him guide you. Learn from His example. See His compassion for the lost. Learn the art of soul winning from the Master. He is all around you, above you, before you, underneath you—so commune with Him daily.

In addition to learning from Jesus, be mentored by a pastor or leader in your church. The ministry of the soul winner or evangelist will contribute much to the growth of the local church, but you must be under the cover of a pastor. An evangelist can be used of God particularly effectively if under the authority of a pastor and a local church. I have talked with some good soul winners and they are doing great works, but those that are not under any form of authority need to consider the spiritual principle of mentorship. Even some great evangelists who shook nations but refused to be under authority ended up in error. We can learn from their mistakes. You need to be mentored as well, as Paul mentored Timothy, and Elijah mentored Elisha. Get a mentor; no man is an island.

We need to be accountable to God and to each other. Evangelistic activities that are endorsed, initiated, and supported by the local church will have the greatest blessing of God. Don't be proud. God resists the proud. Instead, be humble. God lifts the humble.

The trouble is, some churches and pastors do not hold the ministry of the evangelist in high esteem. I have met some pastors who, perhaps because of some negative experience in the past with evangelists, do not like evangelists and are not encouraging those in their congregations who wish to perform that ministry. I wish that every pastor and every church in the land highly regarded the ministry of the evangelist or soul winner. While some evangelists don't want to submit because they have been wounded, some pastors don't want evangelists because they too have been wounded. In time, God will heal them both. They will work together hand in hand.

So to be effective in soul winning, as in Christian leadership, one must have the essential qualifications: be a keen student of the Bible. Live a clean lifestyle. maintain a strong prayer life, courage, perseverance, willingness to change, and willingness to learn. We also believe that being born again is a prerequisite for soul winning. As Dwight L. Moody said, "I have never known anyone who is successful in soul winning who does not have the assurance of his own salvation." I have come to the conclusion that effective evangelism, especially discipleship and friendship evangelism, succeeds or fails depending on the life and character of the messenger, for the messenger is the real book that people read.

Chapter 4

The Holy Spirit in Evangelism

Do not get drunk with wine, for that is dissipation, but be filled with the Spirit. Ephesians 5:18.

The Holy Spirit is the giver of life to the dead, the great emancipator from sin, the great energizer for the Christian, the divine agent that makes evangelism possible. When you are filled with the Holy Spirit, you can shout and say like Paul, "I can do all things through Him who strengthens me" (Philippians 4:13). Without the Holy Spirit, evangelism fails. Without the Holy Spirit, tackling objections will prove impossible, the Word of God will remain closed, the evangelist's message will become boring, the unregenerate will remain lost, and salvation will be unattainable.

It is God's command that Christians "be filled with the Spirit" (Ephesians 5:18). That means to come under the influence and control of the Holy Spirit, to act, talk, and do things in ways that are not your own. The only way you can become effective and productive in evangelism is by being filled with the Holy Spirit. The Spirit empowers Christians for works of service and makes them dynamic in witnessing (Acts 1:8) and able to perform wonders and miraculous signs for the glory of God (Acts 2:43). The Spirit makes Christians of one heart and mind with other believers (Acts 4:32) and devoted to worship and teaching (Acts 2:42). This is the same Spirit who came on the day of Pentecost, the day the church was born. It's the same Holy Spirit who baptizes every believer in the Body of Christ (I Corinthians 12:3), the same Spirit who performed all those mighty acts through human beings recorded in the book of Acts and today.

Salvation is a work of the Holy Spirit of God alone. God uses the preacher—but it's the Holy Spirit who produces salvation. Jesus makes this plain in the Scriptures: "unless one is born of water and the Spirit he cannot enter into the kingdom of God" (John 3:5-8); "It is the Spirit who gives life; the flesh profits nothing" (John 6:63). And in Titus 3:5-6, Paul tells us how God "saved us...by the washing of regeneration and renewing by the Holy Spirit, whom He poured out upon us richly through Jesus Christ our Savior." Finally, the Lord gives us this sobering teaching in John 6:65: "no one can come to Me unless it has been granted him from the Father." The Father brings sinners to Himself only through the Holy Spirit, who proceeds from the Father and the Son.

You need to be filled with the Holy Spirit to be used mightily of God in power evangelism. You must sense your complete powerlessness without Him. It's the Holy Spirit Who helps Christians in their infirmities, (Romans 8:16), gives us the assurance that we are born again (Romans 8:16), and aids us in our prayer life (Jude 20). The Spirit is the source of power for witnessing and discipleship (Acts 1:8), and the fountain of all spiritual life (John 4:13-14). The results of being filled with the Holy Spirit are speaking the Word of God with all boldness (Acts 4:31), godly character (Galatians 5:22-23), supernatural gifts of healing, faith, and working of miracles (1Corinthians 12:1-16).

The need to be filled with the Holy Spirit is greater than ever. Baptism and infilling of the Spirit are two distinct ministries of the Spirit in the life of the believer. The infilling work and ministry of the Holy Spirit is the fundamental of fundamentals in Pentecostal, Charismatic and Renewal theology. Unfortunately, the current trend in many churches is to neglect to preach on this tenet of their faith. Here we will confine ourselves to the infilling of the Holy Spirit. The Holy Spirit filling ministry has been classified into the following.

The General Filling Ministry.

This is particularly important as it relates to Christians coming under the control of the Holy Spirit unreservedly and yielding themselves to God (Romans 12:1-2). This makes it possible to be "clean pipes" through which God's blessings can stream and pour forth. The first condition of usefulness in God's ministry is cleanliness. God looks neither for qualifications nor ordinations—He looks for clean people. The general filling of the spirit leads Christians into growth and maturity. Some Christians are not maturing. Stop and ask yourself: am I growing? Evaluate your own spiritual growth. Renounce every idol. Confess every sin and repent. Then experience the general filling ministry of the Spirit for your own spiritual growth and development. "But I say, walk by the Spirit, and you will not carry out the desire of the flesh." (Galatians 5:16).

The Special Filling Ministry.

This relates to the special endowment of the Holy Spirit to perform special functions. It's this filling that came on Peter and others on the day of Pentecost when they were filled with the Holy Spirit when they spoke (Acts 2:4, 4:8, 4:31). As you remember, that special filling resulted in three thousand people being saved in one day. In this time, too, we must be filled with the Holy Spirit in a unique and special way.

We should not be dogmatic about these two filling ministries of the Holy Spirit, as some Christians are unfamiliar with the distinction. So whether you recognize the special and general filling as distinct is not an essential matter. The essential matter is that you must be filled with the Holy Spirit. Do not engage in discipleship without daily filling. Do not presume that just because you were filled yesterday, you are filled today. Ask God to fill you with His Spirit every day.

The Bible teaches the necessity for being filled with the Holy Spirit to produce great results. There are many who preach without much impact, but the problem is not their speaking style. God is not looking for orators. He's not looking for entertainers; there are already plenty of those. He's not interested in our abilities, but in our availabilities. He's looking for ordinary, humble Christians who are filled with the Holy Spirit and through whom He can perform humanly impossible miracles. God is interested in spirit-filled men and women who will do the works that Jesus did by the power of the Holy Spirit. God is looking for people who will preach under the anointing and through whom He will perform miracles, signs and wonders that are extraordinary. God is looking for doers. He's looking for shakers and changers, a new breed who will preach radically, exercising power and authority like Jesus did until sinners exclaim, "What is this? A new teaching with authority!" (Mark 1:27).

What role does being filled with the Holy Spirit play in evangelism? This is an important question. Spirit-filled Christians will be mightily empowered by God to do things beyond their human ability and comprehension. They will perform signs and wonders. Wonders are mighty acts of God whereby He causes people to stand in awe of Him and to wonder. When the Holy Spirit came suddenly on the day of the Pentecost as a mighty rushing wind, it was the wonder that caused the city to come in bewilderment. All were perplexed; they had to find out what was happening. Curiosity drew the crowd, and three thousand people were converted. The church today needs to regain the signs and wonders that were prevalent in the first-century church. Great things take place when you evangelize through the power of the Holy Spirit. People will be amazed at the powerful words that you speak. They will be astonished at the miracles that God will perform through you. Acts such as these made Nicodemus confess of Christ, "we know that You have come from God as a teacher; for no one can do these signs that You do unless God is with him" (John 3:2). Soul winners empowered by the Holy Spirit will affect many lives.

"These signs will accompany those who have believed: in My name they will cast out demons, they will speak with new tongues; they will pick up serpents, and if they drink any deadly poison, it will not hurt them; they will lay hands on the sick, and they will recover" (Mark 16:17-18). The preaching of the Word will go out with great velocity when accompanied by signs. Signs are pointers to someone else who is coming. Mark 16:17-18, quoted above, despite being the source of skepticism among some textual critics and elite scholars in regard to the authenticity of the authorship, is a key text for Pentecostal preaching. To those of us who accept this portion of the Scripture as infallible and authoritative, it has become a living creature, a part of all we preach and practice. It's the trademark of a truly dynamic ministry to all who will be used of the Holy Spirit in power evangelism. Briefly stated, the Lord enumerated five powerful signs that were meant to go hand in hand with the proclamation of the Gospel:

1. Casting out devils.
2. Speaking with new tongues.
3. Picking up serpents with their hands (not literally, but figuratively).
4. Not being hurt by deadly poison.
5. Healing of the sick.

"Many wonders and signs were taking place through the apostles" (Acts 2:43). The coming of the Holy Spirit on the day of Pentecost (Acts 2) enabled the early church to propagate the

Gospel and bring glory to God by the signs that followed them. We learn that signs pointed the people not to the evangelists, but to the Lord who was working through them. The concept of following signs needs to accompany us wherever and whenever we preach. Any church or individual that has lost this trademark must seek God for a fresh outpouring of the Holy Spirit.

The Old and New Testaments are full of people who performed many miracles through the Holy Spirit. It's necessary today to demonstrate the Gospel by valid and documented miracles. Elijah and Elishah performed great miracles; Stephen did "great wonders and signs" (Acts 6:8). Peter performed many miracles; even when his shadow was cast on sick people, they were healed. He raised Tabitha from the dead, and this great miracle became well known and caused many people to come to faith. Of the Apostle Paul it is said that "God was performing extraordinary miracles by the hands of Paul, so that handkerchiefs or aprons were even carried from his body to the sick, and the diseases left them and the evil spirits went out" (Acts 19:11-12). The early church was a spirit-filled church. Things were happening, and not only among the Apostles. God also used ordinary church folk like Stephen. Jesus Himself taught that these signs should follow "those who have believed" (Mark 16:17)—not just the clergy, but *all* who believe.

How can I be filled with the Holy Spirit? If you are truly hungry and thirsty for the Spirit, you will be filled. The Holy Spirit will come upon you when you have confessed and repented of every sin (Acts 2:31). The Spirit will then work in your life to produce cleanliness and godliness. Some of the scriptural conditions for the infilling of the Holy Spirit are that you yield yourself to God (Romans 12:1-2), give yourself to prayer (Acts 4:31), and walk in obedience to God (Acts 5:32). The Holy Spirit will come upon you if you study

29

the Scriptures and allow yourself to be saturated by them (John 6:63), walk free from sin (Romans 6:11-13), and ask God to fill you with the Holy Spirit by believing (Galatians 3:2, James 1:5, Matthew 7:9).

Words Of Knowledge.

The gift of words of knowledge can be a vital part of evangelism. Because Christians too often underestimate the importance of the gifts of the Holy Spirit in evangelism, words of knowledge are often overlooked in evangelism lectures at theological seminaries. Here we shall attempt to give a general overview of some of the scriptural teachings on the gift of words of knowledge, so as to grasp and understand more fully and correctly this special gift of the Holy Spirit.

Words of knowledge refers to the special gift bestowed on some believers by the Holy Spirit as He wills, enabling them to have accurate and detailed knowledge of things and events which they could not otherwise have known. If it is your gift, use it in evangelism and everywhere else. *Accurate* words of knowledge will no doubt make a profound impact on the inquirer. But use them always at the right time and in the right way. Also, obviously not all who set out to evangelize are gifted in using words of knowledge, and attempting to use words of knowledge when you do not have the gift ends in failure.

Bear in mind some important points about the gift of words of knowledge.

• God gives this special gift through the power of the Holy Spirit, and we must rely on the Spirit as the source of our knowledge in order to hear His voice. Since the Holy Spirit knows all things, we can rely on Him to show us events and details about the inquirer. This will further enable us to communicate the Gospel as we address their specific need.

• The Holy Spirit imparts the gift on believers sovereignly, therefore there is no rule that all believers can be so gifted.

•   Those who are gifted must have accurate and detailed knowledge of the events, person, or things revealed to them. This is necessary to avoid mere guessing, or worse, heresy. Accuracy is an absolute necessity for operating in words of knowledge. Without accuracy, the message will be treated with contempt, as little better than a parlor game. Accurate words of knowledge will touch the heart of the hearer, causing them to marvel, *How did they know all this about me?* Their next thought will be, *If they know about me, maybe this message is true!* When people begin to think and ask the right questions, the way of salvation starts to open.

I have rejoiced at the tremendous response when God chooses to give me words of knowledge for specific people and at specific times. On one occasion, I was on a train from Nynashamn to Stockholm in Sweden. The Holy Spirit gave me words of knowledge in four specific areas about a man who was sitting in front of me. I had never met the man before. I didn't know where he was from. I didn't even know his name. He just sat in front of me on the train. But I knew God was speaking to me about him. I tried to put it off. I told myself it was all a product of my imagination. I had never operated in words of knowledge when dealing with unbelievers before, and I did not want to speak to that man!

I began to feel uncomfortable. Soon I was so pressed by the Spirit that I looked the man in the eye and told him the four things God revealed to me about him:

1)   That he had received an expensive watch as a gift from a friend in Switzerland;

2)   That he had been married twice before and that the marriage he was currently in was going through a crisis which threatened to dissolve it;

3)   That his business was prospering but he had once had a business partner who had taken advantage of him,

ripped him off, and moved to Norway;

4)   And that when he was 18 years old, he was sexually abused and he needed to repent and forgive.

When I finished pronouncing the words, the man began to cry, and asked me to pray for him to receive Jesus Christ as Lord and Savior. He verified that every word was accurate.

I had resisted, but all I needed was to have faith, and declare in faith what I felt to be the word of the Lord. We need a great deal of faith so we can be used of God in words of knowledge, because when we get the words we are prone to doubting. We ask ourselves, *Is this from me or from God?* That type of reasoning often hinders us first from believing that God is speaking to us, and then from overcoming our fears and speaking aloud the wonderful words of knowledge. Don't be afraid of getting it wrong. There are no experts in words of knowledge. We all get it wrong at times, and we learn from our mistakes. Overcome fear by speaking out!

Biblical Basis For Words Of Knowledge.

From the very beginning of His ministry, we have an indication that the Lord Jesus used accurate words of knowledge to convict people of their sin, speak to their pain, and draw them to saving faith in Him.

Earlier we cited the case of Nathanael. Jesus knew all about him. "Jesus saw Nathanael coming to Him, and said of him, 'Behold, an Israelite indeed, in whom there is no deceit!'

Nathanael said to Him, 'How do You know me?' Jesus answered and said to him, 'Before Philip called you, when you were under the fig tree, I saw you.'

Nathanael answered Him, 'Rabbi, You are the Son of God; You are the King of Israel.'" (John 1:47-49).

Jesus' words of knowledge caused an amazed Nathanael to confess Jesus as the Son of God. Another example is the Samaritan woman at the well. The Lord revealed to her the unpleasant truth about herself, facts that she could not refute.

During their short conversation at the well, she said to him that she had no husband. Imagine her surprise when Jesus calmly caught her in this little fib: "You have correctly said, 'I have no husband'; for you have had five husbands, and the one whom you now have is not your husband; this you have said truly" (John 4:17). Confused, she said, "Sir, I perceive that You are a prophet." Her amazement only grew when Jesus declared to her that He was not a prophet, He was the Messiah, the Christ. She left Him, wondering—but we read of her going to her friends and family saying, "Come, see a man who told me all the things that I have done; this is not the Christ, is it?" And all this is because He told her things He could not have known from any source other than the Holy Spirit.

A word of knowledge can often pave the way for salvation. Words of knowledge are not necessary for salvation, but we must be open to receiving this gift. The Scriptures endorse using words of knowledge if one is so gifted (1 Corinthians 13:8, 1 Corinthians 12:8). We know the gift of the word of knowledge is in existence today, and we often hear of it. In fact, in some circles it's becoming popular to evangelize by this method. This type of evangelism, referred to by some as "prophetic evangelism," has given some Christians previously uninvolved in evangelism a new power and zeal.

Nothing in Scripture or in our study indicates that signs, wonders, and words of knowledge were only endowed on Jesus or the first century Apostles. They are also to accompany the preaching of the Gospel today. What do you do now? Ask God in faith to fill you with His Holy Spirit so that you can be used mightily in power evangelism. The Holy Spirit will lead you to the right person, at the right time and the right place, and will give you the right words to say, to share God's message in the way that He wants you to, and cause the inquirer to respond accordingly. The Spirit convicts the inquirer of sin, of righteousness, and of judgement (John 16:8) and opens the listener's heart to the message (Acts 16:14). Walk in the Spirit, live in the Spirit, be led by the Spirit, be filled by the Spirit, be moved by the Spirit, and controlled by the Spirit. When you are so possessed by the Spirit, then you will be so possessed by God Himself, living in the presence of God. "Not by might nor by power, but by My Spirit,' says the LORD of hosts" (Zechariah 4:6). Glory to God!

Chapter 5

The Message of Salvation

The evangelist is the messenger, and the core of the message is the Gospel, the means of salvation. Soul winners, personal evangelists, and all Christian workers have a responsibility and a mandate to deliver this message. They must be ever mindful that it is not their message, but God's: "we do not preach ourselves but Christ Jesus as Lord, and ourselves as your bond-servants for Jesus' sake" (2 Corinthians 4:5). This demands that the message be delivered in integrity and faithfulness.

The message to be heralded is the message of repentance, faith, and Jesus Christ. It is not possible to be saved without these things. Paul wrote in his farewell address to the Ephesian elders of "testifying to both Jews and Greeks of repentance toward God and faith in our Lord Jesus Christ." (Acts 20:21). Any gospel that does not lead to repentance and faith in Jesus Christ crucified is not the true Gospel.

Repentance.

Repentance is one criterion for forgiveness of sins. All must repent; those who have not repented will not be let into heaven. Thus there is an urgent need to preach repentance today, just as in Jesus' day. John the Baptist came as God's messenger, preaching the message of repentance: "Repent, for the kingdom of heaven is at hand" (Matthew 3:2). Or as Jesus Himself said in Mark 1:15: "The time is fulfilled, and the kingdom of God is at hand; repent and

35

believe in the gospel." As the message of the evangel is proclaimed, repentance and faith spring up in the hearer. The door of salvation opens to the repentant.

In considering what repentance *is,* let's start with a few things that it *isn't.*

Reformation.

Turning over a new leaf.

Regret/fear of being caught.

Doing good works.

Mere intellectual assent.

While some or all of these things may play a part, true repentance is much more. Natural feelings or remorse are not genuine repentance. Many people seem to have repented, but afterwards regress. It's possible that those who regress didn't experience real repentance in the first place. They may have wept, fasted, and been prayed over, but never actually experienced true repentance. If life is not changed, real repentance is absent. If repentance has not been experienced, salvation has not been experienced.

"The kindness of God leads you to repentance." (Romans 2:4). Only the Holy Spirit can produce real repentance. If one is not careful in evangelism, one may deceive people unwittingly. To lead people to a place of making decisions without proper repentance is like taking bread out of the oven before it's properly baked. We'll not produce genuine disciples this way. In crusades I have sometimes heard altar calls like this one: "If you want to go to heaven, put up your hand!" Such altar calls may at times seem 100% successful— who doesn't want to go to heaven? But they might have few genuine conversions. If repentance is not preached, sin exposed, and Jesus proclaimed as Savior and Deliverer, the message falls short. We must first lead the unregenerate to a place of repentance from sin and faith in the Lord Jesus before we can lead them to a place of making decisions. They must know what they are doing.

When dealing with an inquirer, don't try to force a quick decision. Ask if they are ready. Show them in the Scriptures that now is the time and this is the day of salvation, for we never know what tomorrow may bring (II Corinthians 6:2; Proverbs 27:1). If they are not ready, be patient. Smile, remain friendly, pray with them. Remember, it's not your message. He Who sent you commands that repentance should be preached, and you must do it in His time.

So…what is repentance? The Greek word for repentance is *metanoia*: a change (meta) of mind (noia). Thus in repentance we turn to a new direction. The three specific areas about which we should change our minds are God, sin, and ourselves.

God. St Augustine of Hippo said, "Every man has a vacuum in his soul and is restless until that vacuum is filled by God." Everyone has an emptiness within them, and the unregenerate tries in vain to fill that vacuum with wealth, possessions, and things of this life. In repentance we truly see God, a Holy God, a God who loves us, a God who cares for us, a God who wants to have fellowship with us and bring us to heaven. As we repent, God changes our mind about Him. All our thoughts and concepts about Him change. All our old questions—"Why? Why me? Why am I feeling this pain? If God loves the world, why is there so much suffering?"—all these questions dissolve, because our mind is set on God. We accept that God is who He says He is, that He means what He says, and that He will do what He says He will do. We let go of all our misconceptions about God, and approach Him as our Father.

"Father, I have sinned against heaven and in your sight. I am no longer worthy to be called your son" (Luke 15:21). In repentance we acknowledge our sins before God, as did the Prodigal Son, but we can do so with the assurance that our Father will forgive us, joyfully accepting us as His children.

Sin. Repentance changes our mind about sin, and leads to confession of sins. It was when John the Baptist preached on repentance that all around him confessed their sins and were baptized (Matthew 3:6). When the Gospel is preached, sinners see sin as it really is, that which is malignantly evil, that which torments, humiliates, brings shame and filthiness. They may once have loved sin and enjoyed its pleasures, but now they feel remorse; they hate sin with perfect hatred.

The subject of sin is not taught in some churches. Some ministers avoid preaching on sin, thinking it too offensive. However, this issue must be dealt with before one can come to saving faith. Sin is the thing that hurts a Christian the most. If someone claims to be a Christian and enjoys sin, that person is under self-deception. A repentant person chooses not to live as they did before, and will adopt new behaviors and lifestyle. God grants us real repentance so that we can turn completely from our sin. John Wesley declared, "Give me seven men who love God with all their hearts and fear nothing but sin, and I will turn the world upside down."

Ourselves. "For all have sinned and fall short of the glory of God...." (Romans 3:23). God's word clearly declares that all have sinned. Man was born in sin, lives in sin, and continues in sin. Many people do charitable works, and there are many who argue that all who do such good works will go to heaven. However, the only criteria for going to heaven are repenting and accepting Jesus as Lord and Savior. Anyone who misses this fact will miss heaven. Nicodemus (John 3) very nearly missed it. Cornelius was a good man, but Peter had to preach to him so that he could be saved (Acts 10). The Pharisees were such good religious people that even Jesus commended them for their righteousness (Matthew 5:20), but they failed to accept Jesus for Who He is. The thief on the cross, on the other hand, though he was a violent robber, saw Jesus and knew Him, and repented. Jesus said to this man, "Truly I say to you, today you shall be with Me in Paradise." (Luke 23:43). This thief, whose good works had been few if any, was with Our Lord that very day—all because he admitted his sins, repented, and accepted Jesus Christ as his Savior.

In considering the above, it pays to answer true or false to the following statements.

I am a Christian because I go to church. Wrong! Visiting a foreign country doesn't make you a citizen (Philippians 3:20). Nicodemus was a good man, but Jesus told him, "Truly, truly, I say to you, unless one is born again he cannot see the kingdom of God...unless one is born of water and the Spirit he cannot enter into the kingdom of God" (John 3:3, John 3:5). You become a citizen of heaven by being born anew! No matter how good a person you are, no matter how involved in your church, without repentance, you're still a sinner.

I am a Christian because I was born into a Christian family or in a Christian country. Wrong! Being in a garage doesn't make you a car. Salvation is an individual matter: "choose for yourselves today whom you will serve" (Joshua 24:15).

I am a Christian because I am charitable. Wrong! The Pharisees were charitable, but Jesus condemned them for their hardness of heart. Cornelius gave money, but he still needed to repent. Paul taught that our works count for nothing if we lack the love that is in Christ: "If I give all my possessions to feed the poor, and if I surrender my body to be burned, but do not have love, it profits me nothing" (1 Corinthians 13:3).

I am a Christian because I am a good person. Wrong! Good people are not good all the time. It takes only one sin to make a sinner; maybe even one thought, a little anger in a traffic jam. God sent His Son to earth precisely because no one is good enough to earn salvation: "We have believed in Christ Jesus, so that we may be justified by faith in Christ and not by the works of the Law; since by the works of the

Law no flesh will be justified" (Galatians 2:16).

Real repentance touches and changes all our faculties: intellect, emotion, and will. That all faculties are activated and touched is explained in Scripture and demonstrated in both the stories of Jonah and the Ninevites, and the Prodigal Son.

Intellect. "Then Jonah began to go through the city one day's walk; and he cried out and said, 'Yet forty days and Nineveh will be overthrown.' Then the people of Nineveh believed in God" (Jonah 3:4-5). At the preaching of Jonah, the Ninevites changed their mind—and a good thing, too! The role of intellect in repentance is also well illustrated in the Parable of the Prodigal Son. After squandering his inheritance and living among swine—about the lowest one could go in Hebrew culture—his intellect kicked in. "He came to his senses" (Luke 15:17).

The Gospel must appeal to the intellect. Knowing a person's way of thinking is key—people must be reached at their level, allowing them to think over the Gospel message in a way that makes sense to them.

Some people ask, "Can the mentally ill, whose intellectual faculty is affected, come to their senses? If not, can they be saved? Can someone who is under the influence of drugs or alcohol be converted in their state? How about demoniacs?" In the case of mental illness, we present the Gospel and pray. As we do, God's Holy Spirit is able to touch the afflicted person. As salvation is a work of God, God can reach the person where he or she is in terms of intellectual faculties. The same is true of those under the influence. Though it may seem futile at the time, God may be at work in them. And demoniacs, as in Jesus' day, need deliverance and forgiveness to be administered.

Emotion. "When the word reached the king of Nineveh, he arose from his throne, laid aside his robe from him, covered himself with sackcloth and sat on the ashes" (Jonah 3:6). Sackcloth and dust or ashes were a symbol of mourning. The Ninevites *wore* their repentance. It is likely that the Prodigal Son wore his repentance as well—the Gospel indicates that he got straight up from the pigpen and set off to his father's house. He was almost certainly covered with manure, food scraps, and dust from his journey by the time he reached his father, and his words suggest that he was in despair. And so repentance includes feelings of contrition and sorrow as we face our sins and bring them before our Father.

Will. Before people are pressured to make the decision for Christ, their intellect and emotions must have been appealed to, or they won't really know what they're in for. The decision won't truly be their own. The Ninevites heard and believed Jonah's message, then felt remorse. Only then did they take action: they "turned from their wicked way" (Jonah 3:10). God saw this and had mercy on them. The experience of the Prodigal Son was similar. He saw his predicament and went to his father, despairing, not expecting to be treated as a son, but only hoping his father would give him a job so he wouldn't starve. After his intellect and emotions were engaged, he made his plan and carried it out, even after his father joyfully embraced him: "Father, I have sinned against heaven and in your sight. I am no longer worthy to be called your son" (Luke 15:21). But his father rejoiced at the return of his son, and all was forgiven, as our Heavenly Father rejoices when we repent and return to Him.

We must faithfully preach repentance as our Lord commanded it. As we do so, others will be cut to the heart by the message we proclaim. They will cry out, "What must we do to be saved?" We will lead them to repentance by appealing to their intellect, emotion, and will, causing the inquirer to change his mind about God, sin, and himself.

Faith.

Repentance paves the way for faith in the Lord Jesus, which is essential to conversion. Faith and repentance co-exist in conversion. We are saved not by repentance alone, but by grace through faith, having repented of our sins. Faith is a gift from God, as Paul declared in Ephesians 2:8: "For by grace you have been saved through faith; and that not of yourselves, it is the gift of God."

There are different types of faith; however, we will look at saving faith. Here are some definitions:

• Faith is being sure of what we hope for and certain of what we do not see. Hebrews 11:1

• Forsaking All I Trust Him!

• "An active trusting obedience and never apart from divine revelation." Professor Bruce Busch.

• Faith is trusting in God, taking Him at His word.

Saving faith comes into the sinners' heart as the soul winner proclaims the Word. The Word of God expressly teaches us that faith is a product of hearing. It's in the preaching that the unregenerate come to an understanding of God's Word.

Romans 10:14-18 gives us God's order and strategy for soul winning. There are five steps to leading souls to a saving faith.

Step 1: Church Or Mission. This is the foundational and most important stage. Churches and missions are needed to commission soul winners. Without senders—the church or mission—evangelistic activities will be hindered. Many are failing to win souls simply because the senders have not trained and motivated them. "How will they preach unless they are sent?" (Romans 10:15).

Step 2: Preaching. The soul winner, having been sent by God through the church or mission, goes and preaches Good News. Appointed to herald the Gospel, he or she must work hard preaching the Gospel, which is the divinely ordained means of salvation.

Step 3: Hearing. "Faith comes from hearing, and hearing by the word of Christ" (Romans 10:17). People hear the Word through personal witnessing, testimony, or other methods of evangelism. As they listen, faith begins to well up within them. Without preaching there would be no hearing, and without the local church or mission agency there would be no preaching.

Step 4: Believing. Because faith comes by hearing the word of God, it's not possible for sinners to believe without hearing, and they cannot hear unless someone preaches or witnesses or evangelizes. When they believe, they are ready to receive the Lord Jesus.

Step 5: Calling. "Whoever will call on the name of the Lord will be saved" (Romans 10:13). This is the ultimate stage, because they have heard and they have believed, and are now able to call on the Lord for salvation. They cannot call before they believe. They cannot believe before they hear. They cannot hear before the preaching. There cannot be preaching before the preachers are sent. There cannot be sending unless the church initiates.

Since saving faith is believing faith, the inquirer has to trust in Christ and in Him alone as the only ground for salvation. This may appear simple at face value, but not all people can obtain it. When we exercise saving faith in God, we place everything into His hands. We trust Him. We transfer our trust from ourselves or anything else to Christ. This can be humbling, even frightening, but it also brings a glorious peace.

The essence of saving faith is that it is in God. In the message of the evangel, one is born again simply by believing in the Lord Jesus Christ.

Jesus Christ.

The message of the messenger calls for repentance and faith. Repentance is Godward. Faith is toward the Lord Jesus Christ. (Acts 20:21).

Christianity hinges on the uniqueness of Christ. I want to reiterate that Jesus Christ is the central theme of the evangel, for the mystery of our Christian faith rests on the incarnation of Christ, who "was revealed in the flesh, was vindicated in the Spirit, seen by angels, proclaimed among the nations, believed on in the world, taken up in glory" (1Timothy 3:16)." We believe that Jesus Christ is God incarnate; we believe that for our sake, Jesus Christ, "who, although He existed in the form of God, did not regard equality with God a thing to be grasped, but emptied Himself, taking the form of a bond-servant, and being made in the likeness of men. Being found in appearance as a man, He humbled Himself by becoming obedient to the point of death, even death on a cross" (Philippians 2: 6-8).

We believe that Jesus Christ was conceived of and born to a virgin. We believe that, though sinless, He died a substitutionary death and descended into hell. We believe He arose from the dead, ascended into heaven and will come again to judge the living and the dead. We believe His kingdom will have no end.

The deity of Jesus Christ, while fully man, is endorsed by the Holy Scriptures (1 Timothy 2:5, Mark 10:45). Anyone who says He was merely a teacher or a moral example is wrong. Those who do not accept that Jesus is God in flesh are wrong (John 1:14). Jesus was 100% man. He was hungry, He was thirsty, He was tired, He was sorrowful. However, at the same time, Jesus was 100% God. The divinity of Christ as the second Person of the Trinity must be acknowledged. He was and still is, in the words of the Nicene creed AD 325, revised at Constantinople AD 381, "God of God, Light of Light, Very God of Very God, begotten, not made, being of the same substance with the Father." We can neither comprehend nor fathom this mystery, but we accept by faith that Jesus is God and Jesus is man.

Why is Jesus Christ the central theme of the evangel? Our salvation proceeds from Him. All Christological teachings reveal that only by believing in Christ and Him alone are we saved from sin and death. He had to be born of a virgin and conceived of the Holy Spirit so that He could be the Paschal Lamb, to expiate the sin of the whole world. He had to be fully man to be a rightful high priest, touched by the feelings of our infirmities. He had to be human and yet without sin in order to bear our sins. God required a perfect sacrifice.

The heart of the evangel rests in three words: the *death*, *burial*, and *resurrection* of Jesus Christ. No one can receive salvation outside of Jesus Christ.

Death. The message of the cross always provokes. Can God die? The idea of God dying on the cross for His creation challenges logic, and there have always been disputes on the subject. Some cannot accept an apparently weak God Who did not defend Himself. Unaided by the Holy Spirit, we may not believe that God "humbled Himself by becoming obedient to the point of death, even death on a cross" (Philippians 2). "For the word of the cross is foolishness to those who are perishing," wrote the Apostle Paul in I Corinthians 1:18, "but to us who are being saved it is the power of God." Christ possessed two natures; He was both fully God and fully man. As God He never ceased to exist, but as man He had to die to redeem us. This death we must accept and preach.

He died a unique death. He did not deserve to die; even Pilate declared three times, "I find no fault in Him!" He took our place in death. For salvation we come to the foot of the cross where we see Him carrying our burden of sin: God "made Him who knew no sin to be sin on our behalf, so that we might become the righteousness of God in Him" (II Corinthians 5:21).

But did Jesus have to die on the cross? Some argue that the cross was not necessary, that Jesus could have died in a car crash and still achieved our salvation—what counts is the shed blood. However, the Bible clearly teaches that Jesus had to die on the cross to fulfill Scripture. The cross was the most horrible form of punishment. It was at the cross that He suffered sacrificially (Isaiah 53). The curse of our sins could not possibly have been removed without the cross (Galatians 3:13, Deuteronomy 21:23).

Burial. As we saw Him on the cross taking our punishment, we pleaded for pardon, "Father forgive." Then, in the darkest hour the world ever knew, He was buried. The burial of Jesus gives us our full identity with Him, for as He was laid in the tomb, so too were our sins.

Resurrection. "We believe in Him who raised Jesus our Lord from the dead, He who was delivered over because of our transgressions, and was raised because of our justification" (Romans 4: 24-25). The resurrection of Jesus Christ demonstrates God's awesome power. Jesus rose from the dead!

Today some liberal theologians advocate that one can be a Christian without believing in the resurrection. However, our Christian faith hinges on the resurrection as on nothing else. If the life and works of Jesus had ended at the grave, people would have thought of Jesus as nothing more than a good man. There would be no Gospel, no justification, no eternal life.

The Scriptures constantly teach the importance of the resurrection. The Lord taught that He would be resurrected from the dead, and by raising Him, God vindicated Him (Romans 1:3-4). Paul instructed the Roman Christians that to be saved, they must believe God raised Jesus from the dead (Romans 10:9). And to the Corinthians, Paul spoke very plainly about the resurrection:

> *"But if there is no resurrection of the dead, not even Christ has been raised; and if Christ has not been raised, then our preaching is vain, your faith also is vain. Moreover we are even found to be false witnesses of God, because we testified against God that He raised Christ, whom He did not raise, if in fact the dead are not raised...and if Christ has not been raised, your faith is worthless; you are still in your sins. Then those also who have fallen asleep in Christ have perished."* (I Corinthians 15:13-15, 17-18).

But then Paul gives the good news: "But now Christ has been raised from the dead" (I Corinthians 15:20). Without the resurrection, we are lost. With the resurrection, we are saved.

Redemption. "In Him we have redemption through His blood, the forgiveness of our trespasses, according to the riches of His grace..." (Ephesians 1:7). Redemption is the divine act of God whereby He has set us free, purchased us. Our freedom is from the bondage of sin and death (Romans 8); the purchase price was the blood of his dear Son, Jesus.

Justification. "[Jesus] was delivered over because of our transgressions, and was raised because of our justification" (Romans 4:25). Justification is the divine act of God whereby He acquits the sinner and declares Him not guilty of the offences that demanded recompense.

Propitiation. "He Himself is the propitiation for our sins" (I John 2:2). Propitiation means the removal of wrath by the offering of a sacrifice. The unregenerate are under God's wrath (John 3:36); by believing in Jesus, the wrath is removed.

"How can the death, burial and resurrection of Jesus Christ save me in the 21ˢᵗ Century? I wasn't even alive back then?" The answer lies solely in the sovereignty of God. Justification, redemption, propitiation are all divine acts. God has the power to do

what He wills. We can see from the Scriptures that when Adam sinned, all sinned (Romans 5:12). We all suffer the effects of sin, poverty, disease, sorrow, and death. Adam's sin and its consequences passed on to all creation. In other words, it was credited to our account, in the same way that if someone transfers money to your bank account, it will be credited to you without your physical presence at the bank.

From the divine viewpoint, all who believe in Christ's finished work on the cross are set free from sin. Righteousness is credited to their account, just as it was to Abraham: "Abraham believed God, and it was credited to him as righteousness" (Romans 4:3). All who believe have been made righteous through Jesus Christ, and sin and death shall have no power over them.

"When you were dead in your transgressions and the uncircumcision of your flesh, He made you alive together with Him, having forgiven us all our transgressions, having canceled out the certificate of debt consisting of decrees against us, which was hostile to us; and He has taken it out of the way, having nailed it to the cross" (Colossians 2:13-14). Christ cancels the sins of all people in all generations, because all our sins were imputed to Him on the cross. He *was* our sin. We didn't have to physically be at Calvary 2000 years ago to receive salvation. God's way of saving humanity has always been by pointing us to Christ. His way of salvation has not changed. We must look back to what Christ did for us and forward to His coming. This is the message of salvation.

Chapter 6

The State of the Unregenerate

As we allow God to touch us, He will show us humanity's needs. A careful consideration of human nature exhibits our great need for the Gospel. The Scriptures teach the following about the unregenerate.

The Unregenerate Is A Sinner.

It is asserted in both the Old and New Testaments that humans are sinners (Psalm 53:3, Ecclesiastes 7:20, Romans 3:9, Romans 3:23). Adam's original sin was imputed to the whole human race (Romans 5:12-13), and we continue to sin because of our own depraved nature. Not only are humans born in sin; not only is sin imputed to us through Adam. Humans are also sinners by choice. Sin is a deliberate act. Every day we must choose to sin or not to sin.

The sinner stands rightfully condemned before the wrath of God. Our sin is the great chasm between ourselves and God. This is why humanity's greatest need is for a Savior, Jesus Christ, the bridge that brings us to God. As through Adam's sin we are all guilty, so through Christ we can all be made righteous.

The Unregenerate Is Dead.

"And you," Paul wrote to the Ephesian Christians, "were dead in your trespasses and sins, in which you formerly walked according to the course of this world" (Ephesians 2:1). The unregenerate is not physically dead. His or her death is worse than physical; it is a spiritual death. Physical death is a consequence of spiritual death, and both are the result of sin. The second death, also referred to as the lake of fire, will be the final punishment for unrepented sin.

The Scriptures make it plain that anyone who is separated from God is dead. In Genesis 2:17 God warned Adam, "from the tree of the knowledge of good and evil you shall not eat, for in the day that you eat from it you will surely die." We know that Adam did not die the same day that he ate of the forbidden fruit; his physical death came much later. However, he died a spiritual death the instant he disobeyed God. Though the Prodigal Son had not died physically, his father said of him, "this brother of yours was dead and *has begun* to live…" (Luke 15:32). He had not died physically, but spiritually. He was separated from his father. There was no union, no fellowship, no correspondence—nothing between father and son. This was a death, and only by repentance could all be restored.

The greatest of miracles is not when one who has died physically is resurrected. The greatest miracle is when one who has died a spiritual death is resurrected through repentance of sins and belief in Jesus Christ.

The Unregenerate Is Blind.

The unregenerate may not realize that he or she is in need of illumination. The devil has blinded the unregenerate to prevent him or her from believing: "The god of this world has blinded the minds of the unbelieving so that they might not see the light of the gospel of the glory of Christ, who is the image of God" (II Corinthians 4:4).

All the unregenerate's spiritual faculties are impaired. Their eyes are dim; they cannot see the Kingdom of God (John 3:3). Their conscience is dead, their ears are deaf to hearing spiritual truth, and their hearts are closed. Through faithful proclamation of the Gospel, God will "open their eyes so that they may turn from darkness to light and from the dominion of Satan to God" (Acts 26:18).

The Unregenerate Is Lost.

"All of us like sheep have gone astray, each of us has turned to his own way…" (Isaiah 53:6). Like lost sheep, the unregenerate have strayed from God, who is the great Shepherd of sheep. The Father's heart goes out to the lost, and He searches for them diligently. Jesus demonstrated this by being a friend of sinners and publicans. Jesus declared to Zacchaeus, a well-known sinner of the day, "For the Son of Man has come to seek and to save that which was lost" Luke 19:10).

St Augustine of Hippo lived a life of sin and shame. His mother, Monica, had for years faithfully prayed for his conversion. One day, Augustine opened the Bible and his eyes fell on Romans 13:13-14: "Let us behave properly as in the day, not in carousing and drunkenness, not in sexual promiscuity and sensuality, not in strife and jealousy. But put on the Lord Jesus Christ, and make no provision for the flesh in regard to its lusts." Young Augustine was instantly converted upon reading those words. He arose to become one of the best theologians and bishops the church has ever produced.

No one is so lost that they can't be found by God. He can save anyone.

The Unregenerate Is In Satan's Sphere.

We know from the Scriptures that Satan's chief mission is to steal, kill, and destroy (John 10:10), and he works tirelessly to fulfill this goal. It is Satan who seeks to prevent people from hearing the Gospel. He is "the evil one" who catches the seed of the Word that is sown in men's hearts and so hinders them from being saved (Matthew 13:19).

The unregenerate are trapped in Satan's web of deceit, in danger of being taken to hell with him. Through their own sinfulness and under Satan's influence, people sin. As Jesus said bluntly, "You are of your father the devil, and you want to do the desires of your father. He was a murderer from the beginning, and does not stand in the truth because there is no truth in him. Whenever he speaks a lie, he speaks from his own nature, for he is a liar and the father of lies" (John 8:44).

The devil's desire to steal, kill, and destroy has been thwarted by God. Jesus declared, "I came that they may have life, and have it abundantly" (John 10:10). The unregenerate is a child of God, and is God's by right of creation. Satan created no one, died for no one. When Jesus died on the cross, was buried, descended into hell, and rose from the dead on the third day, the great transaction was done. Sinners are reconciled to God. Through the death, burial, and resurrection of Christ, God conquered death, sickness, and the devil.

God's strategy through evangelism is to "open their eyes so that they may turn from darkness to light and from the dominion of Satan to God" (Acts 26:18). We must, in the words of evangelist Reinhardt Bonnke, work at "plundering hell and populating heaven." God will work through us to further His purpose. We must resolve to work tirelessly for God. We must be aggressive. We must go and capture people for Him and bring many to the Kingdom.

The state of the unregenerate compels us to evangelize. You may say, "I have tried it, and failed." Well, now God has called you to succeed. You may have failed many times. So have I. But I have learned from my mistakes. I have also learned that failure is the teacher of success. Success comes to those who have failed and keep on trying. If you never give up, you are a winner.

Keep your head up. Leave your mark on this generation.

Chapter 7

Evangelism: What To Do and What Not To Do

Some succeed in evangelism, and some don't. It depends on one's approach. A fisherman who goes fishing at the wrong time of day, doesn't have a good pole, and doesn't bait his hook, will wait to catch fish in vain. And the fisherman who hasn't even picked up his pole certainly can't expect to catch any fish. We are "fishers of men" (Mark 1:17, Matthew 4:19) and we must learn the art of good fishing. Those who want to be soul winners but haven't tried, must try—that's the most effective way of learning. Theory and practice are two different things, and it's practice that makes the soul winner. It's one thing to know the Gospel, and another to make it known.

We are all different from each other. Because of this, we know that what works for one person may not work for another. However, after working in many countries and across many cultures, in personal evangelism, rallies, conferences, churches, street meetings, and tent campaigns, I humbly present these "Do's and Don'ts of Evangelism." Though I am confident that these principles will work wherever you are, I do not insist upon them. Rather, they are recommended as general guidelines. There are people who memorize one method or style of evangelism and use it on everyone. Some of these professional methods are high-profile and produce great fruits. It's not wrong to use such methods—as long as they *work*.

However, to be truly effective, one must respond to the inquirer's individual thinking so as to touch their emotions, stretch their intellect, and cause their will to respond to Christ. Jesus talked to fishermen in the language of a fisherman, to farmers as a farmer, to Pharisees as a Pharisee. This is one vital rule that will work in evangelism: remember your audience. As Paul says:

> *To the Jews I became as a Jew, so that I might win Jews;*
> *to those who are under the Law, as under the Law...so*
> *that I might win those who are under the Law; to those*
> *who are without law, as without law...so that I might win*
> *those who are without law. To the weak I became weak,*
> *that I might win the weak; I have become all things to all*
> *men, so that I may by all means save some.* (I
> Corinthians 9:20-22).

However, as we have already stressed, there is a need to relax and be yourself when presenting the Gospel. Being all things to all men doesn't mean being artificial or deceitful. It simply means making an effort to reach your inquirer wherever he or she is. Find common ground.

Below are some tips on approaching an inquirer. These have served as guidelines to a number of churches which have implemented and used them in evangelism. Though I will not be legalistic about the don'ts—only the Word of God gives us the blueprint for salvation—first impressions do count, and it is important not to lose the inquirer before you even start.

What Not To Do.

Don't Argue. If the inquirer argues with you, don't argue back. Your duty is to persuade lovingly. Never, ever argue.

Don't Get Side-Tracked. The inquirer may at times seek to divert you or change the subject. Be courteous, but firm.

Pause or make a compliment, and then go back to the main subject. Satan works hard to side-track us. Don't fall for it.

Don't Overdo. Avoid drowning the inquirer in stories and unfamiliar Scripture verses. Use a few relevant verses or illustrations, but stick to the Word. Hit the nail on the head. Be brief.

Don't Rush. Don't finish before you present the whole Gospel. Focus on the death, burial, and resurrection of Jesus. Be sure the inquirer knows what to believe and what not to believe. A Gospel presentation may take 5-10 minutes. If the inquirer is in a hurry, be careful not to become flustered and skip something. Be concise, but take your time. This is the most important decision the inquirer will ever make.

Don't Jargonize. The inquirer may not be familiar with words like born-again, sanctification, or redemption. Avoid using Christian jargon; it could make the inquirer feel excluded.

Don't Be Rude. Never ask, "Don't you understand?" Instead say, "Does this make sense to you?" or "Are you with me?" Never laugh at the inquirer or express surprise at his or her lack of Scriptural knowledge. Use polite language, and monitor your facial expressions and body language. If the inquirer is of a different opinion from you, don't reprimand. Create a friendly atmosphere where you can have an open discussion. Give honest compliments when you can, so you won't come across as harsh.

Don't Be Unkempt. Be presentable. Dress according to the place and culture. You are Christ's witness—look and behave like such a witness.

Don't Get Big-Headed. Sometimes you will meet people who know the Scriptures better than you do. Learn from them. Or someone may ask questions you can't answer. Admit it. There's a saying: "A wise man will sometimes say 'I don't know'." Also, don't become intoxicated by your verbosity. Stay on task. You are a humble servant of the Lord.

Don't Ask Leading Questions. Don't put words in inquirers' mouths, or ask them questions which they will obviously answer in the affirmative: *Do you want to go to heaven? Do you believe God loves you? Do you want to be saved?* If you stop talking and do some listening, people will talk without your talking for them

Don't Hassle. Always compassionately compel inquirers to come to Christ without delay. Make sure they know full Gospel—but let them decide. Don't coerce.

Below are the Do's for the soul winner.

What To Do.

Get To Know The Inquirer. This is the starting point. Don't put on a holy face; talk to the inquirer as you would to someone with whom you are acquainted. In the course of normal conversation, find out about the person: *How have you been? Do you consider yourself religious? How about your family? Do you go to church? Do you think that all good people will go to heaven? In your opinion, how does one become a Christian?* While you don't want it to be an interrogation, these kinds of questions will help you know where the person is coming from and where he or she stands in his or her beliefs. After that, you can present the Gospel properly.

Be Sensitive. Evangelism is listening. The inquirer may be hurting inwardly. Relate by listening to what he or she has to say. When issues such as death, hell, and sin come up, speak with tenderness and compassion.

Tell Them The Problem. Having gotten to know the inquirer, carefully and thoughtfully tell him what the root of the problem is: sin. I emphasize the necessity of telling this *carefully*. Don't withhold explaining that all have sinned, all will die, that our good works are not good enough, and that sin causes separation from God—but tell it with love. If the person is not told carefully, he or she will close up. Explain that the consequences, effects, and results of sin are seen in the world, in homes, in prisons, and in society. Tell how it takes only one sin (even one sinful thought!) to make a sinner. Defining the problem of sin, personalizing the message to the person's life and situation whenever possible, will culminate in the person admitting they have a problem and desiring to know the way of salvation: "what shall we do?" (Acts 2:37).

State The Solution. Once you have examined the problem, show what the solution is. Point the inquirer to the Savior of the world—Jesus, the only One who can deliver us from sin and guilt. Stress this fact: *only Jesus can save from sin.* Emphasize the redemptive work of Jesus Christ at Calvary and implore the inquirer to respond to the love of God, which He demonstrated by sending Jesus Christ.

Call For Action—Now. After the inquirer has realized his or her sinfulness, that God's wonderful plan of salvation is unveiled in Jesus, and that he or she can receive the remedy for sin, ask the inquirer to receive Jesus as Lord and Savior. Explain repentance and ask, "Do you want to repent of your sin and to believe in the Lord Jesus so that you will be saved?" Too often inquirers say, "I want to think about it." Others say "I'll do it later," while still others say "I don't want it." In any case, declare God's verdict: "Now judgment is upon this world" (John 12:31); "Now is 'the acceptable time,' behold, now is 'the day of salvation'" (II Corinthians 6:2).

Pray. For those who make decisions for Christ, lead them into a prayer of salvation. We call this prayer the Repentance Prayer, though it is also known as the Sinner's Prayer. It includes a confession of all sin, an acknowledgement that Jesus died, was buried, and rose from the dead, and an invitation for Jesus to come into their life as Lord and Savior. For those who are not ready, pray for them and with them that the light of the Gospel will penetrate their hearts until they, too, confess Jesus as Lord.

Explain The Christian Life. Tell the new Christian how they

can grow in the faith:
- Read the Word.
- Pray and have communion with God.
- Witness for Jesus.
- Seek fellowship with believers for encouragement and accountability.
- Join a local church, to grow and function in spiritual gifts.

Show Them Discipleship. Love those who have received the Lord, for discipleship begins at this stage. Disciple them so that they can also disciple others (II Timothy 2:2).

Real evangelism and friendship must also be maintained with those who are not yet ready to receive Christ. Show a special love to them, and continue building relationships.

Chapter 8
Obstacles

Not everyone who sets out to evangelize is effective. We can learn more about what works by looking at those who are effective, and seeing what they are putting into practice that others might not be. I would add that in addition to learning from others' successes, we should also learn from the difficulties they encountered. There are obstacles to be expected in evangelism, and an understanding of these obstacles should not deter the soul winner, but prepare him or her for the hindrances to evangelism and to overcome them.

Obstacles.

Fear. Fear is the greatest hindrance to soul winning. Also manifesting itself as "nervousness," it attacks us like a bandit before we witness to the first person. *What will people think about me? What if I look foolish?* Such questioning implies that we're more concerned about other people's opinions about us than what God thinks of us and doing what He has told us to do.

366 times the Bible declares, "Do not fear." Did you know that? That's more than enough for once each day of the year! Thus every day I cast out my fears by love, confessing who I am in Christ. Even so, I get good times and bad times. Some years ago, I was at Speakers Corner in London, preaching to a small crowd of about eight people. When I shouted, "Jesus Christ is Lord!" a teenager came up and spat in my face. I

had never been so embarrassed. I was so angry, I wanted to grab him by the neck and teach him a good lesson in boxing. But when I reached out my hand, God's love filled my heart, pushing out the anger and violence that had been there only moments before. I said to the boy, "I love you so much." He began to cry, repented of his sins, and was converted. As I write this, he is training at Bible College.

So maybe sometimes we do look foolish. I'd rather be a fool for Christ than for the devil. I'd rather be a fool for Christ and witness for Him than do nothing at all. Maybe they'll brand us as fanatics, or lunatics, or fools—let them! We must never be ashamed of Jesus.

What if this person knows me? What if I witness to someone that I rudely pushed as I boarded the train? What if? What if? What if? The fears that can cloud the believer's pathway are innumerable: fear of people, which the Bible prohibits us from having; fear of failure, which prevents us from stepping out and taking risks; imaginary fears of things that will never happen; momentary fears, which arise in an instant and block miracles. Fear of the past. Fear of the future. All these fears are of the devil, because they torment and stop you from walking in faith.

To overcome fear we must have correct thinking through:

1) Renewing our minds (Romans 12:1-2)
2) Fixing our minds on God
3) Believing in ourselves as children of God, and not giving in to self-doubt.

The greatest battles ever fought are in the mind. If the mind speaks fear when there is an opportunity to witness, we can overcome that fear by saying loudly as Jesus did: "It is written." "It is written, 'Let the weak say I am strong.' And it is also written, 'God has not given us a spirit of timidity but of power.'" Your attitude should be as David's: "Be strong and courageous, and act; do not fear nor be dismayed, for the LORD God, my God, is with you" (I Chronicles 28:20).

There is only one fear we should have as Christians, and that is Godly fear. We must stand in awe of God's awesome presence. He is the infinite One, and we are finite; He possesses immortality, and we are mortal; He is the Creator, and we are His creation. We must fear God and serve Him, and Him alone. Look to God instead of yourself. Remember, you are only a vessel. Be careful how you live, but don't let your past affect the present.

Egocentrism.

Many Christians are egocentric instead of Christ-centric. To be egocentric means to be self-centered, while Christ-centric means being Christ-centered. Egocentric people have self on the throne of their hearts. They care about themselves above all others, placing their own convenience above Christian convictions. I have met many egocentric Christians, and while there is no doubt in my mind that they are saved and going to heaven, the sad truth is that they put self first and Christ second. And evangelism? A distant third, or fourth, or even more distant. They may say, "Evangelize? Oh, I can't today. I don't have any time!" The truth is that they have all the time in the world. Perhaps they use family as an escape from Christian duty—"I want to spend time with my family today"—when the fact of the matter is that they will end up on the couch watching television, or in front of the computer, surfing the internet.

The egocentrist has not learned the demands of Jesus: "If anyone wishes to come after Me, he must deny himself, and take up his cross and follow Me" (Mark 8:34). He does not want to pay the cost of discipleship. Egocentric people are lovers of pleasure rather than lovers of God, having plenty of time and money for new cars, new toys and vacations, but not enough money to tithe, and no time to go to worship, no time to pray and read the Bible at home, no time to talk to a soul about Jesus. The egocentrist needs deliverance from the egocentric syndrome. There is truly no excuse for us not to do what God commands.

This attitude of self-centeredness is a major hindrance to Christian witness and evangelism, and Christians need to reconsider where they stand in the matter of self-denial. C.T. Studd once read from the pen of an unbeliever the following words:

> *If I truly, and firmly, and consistently believed as millions say they do, that the knowledge and practice of religion in this life influences destiny in another, religion should be to me everything. I would cast aside every earthly enjoyment as dross, earthly cares as follies and earthly thoughts and feelings as less than vanity. Religion would be my first waking thought, and my last image when sleep sunk me into consciousness.*

Studd was convicted of his own comforts and affluence. He ultimately gave away a large sum of money, founded Worldwide Evangelization Crusade (which operates in many countries today), and sailed as a missionary to China and Africa.

This is but one example of how God can and does transform people from self-centeredness to Christ-centeredness. But He will not do so until they repent and lay everything at the feet of Jesus, and truly seek His kingdom and His righteousness above all other things (Matthew 6:33).

So what is a Christ-centric person? A Christ-centric person is a person with Christ at the center of his or her life, a person who works hard in discipleship, is active in church, and is generous for the cause of Jesus Christ. All that such person has is laid down at the disposal of Jesus. A Christ-centric person reflects the glory of Jesus. This person will not ask, "What would Jesus do in this situation?"—they just do it.

Christ's cause demands your all. Be Christ-centered. Such

are Christians who will impact the lost; they are Christians who, when born to eternal life, will hear the Lord say, "Well done, good and faithful servant. Enter you the joy of your Lord."

Doubt.

There are some questions that can gnaw at the soul winner, making him or her wonder if evangelism is even necessary. Never give in to such doubt. Here are some common questions and their answers.

There is no need for evangelism; God is all-powerful and sovereign. God can accomplish His plan of salvation without us, so He doesn't need our help, right? Well…yes and no. This view holds to the correct Biblical doctrines of omnipotence and sovereignty, but it is nonetheless unscriptural. Of course God doesn't need us—but we are *commanded* to "go…and make disciples" (Matthew 28:19). God's work does not depend upon us, but He has chosen to use us. It is His will to work with and through humanity, using human instruments to accomplish His plans. We must not fail to act. We must obey, whether we like it or not.

The doctrines of omnipotence and sovereignty we embrace, love, and delight in, but we must not use them as an escape from our duty. The Scriptures are as clear on evangelism as they are on sovereignty and omnipotence.

Some countries have already been over-evangelized. This is illogical, unscriptural, and false, and we won't buy it! The whole world needs the Gospel. There is not a single country that has been "over-evangelized." It's not even possible! Some countries have a higher percentage of believers than others, but the need for evangelism is still great. Until everyone accepts Christ, we must keep spreading the Good News.

If God did elect some, not others, to salvation even before time began, then what use is evangelism? This view, also known as predestination, holds that God chose some people and not others to receive salvation. The natural question is: why bother with evangelism, if God has already made His decision?

Whether you believe in divine election or not, there are some salient issues raised. We can study what the Scriptures teach about election. The doctrine of the divine decree of election states: "He chose us in Him before the foundation of the world, that we would be holy and blameless before Him. In love He predestined us to adoption as sons through Jesus Christ to Himself, according to the kind intention of His will" (Ephesians 1:4-5). (See also Romans 8:28-29 and John 10:26-29).

The problem with basing an objection for evangelism and missions on election is that this doctrine does not render evangelistic activities unnecessary. Therefore, those who allege that the elect will be saved even without evangelism have misconstrued the facts. If we hold the view of election, we will also know that it's by preaching of the Gospel that the elect will respond and seal their election. One who holds to election can also hold to the great commission: hold the great commission in the right hand and election in the other, if you will.

It has been said, "The elect don't have an 'E' on their head and the reprobates an 'R'." Therefore, you must preach the Gospel, or you might miss one of the elect! If we accept election, we will also accept the fact that God appointed us, that He will use us as the medium of His salvation.

While I do not here refute the biblical doctrine of election, I reject the idea that the elect will be saved eventually, and that we don't have to reach them. Those who teach so are causing Christians to disobey the Lord's command. Ultimately, whether we believe in election or not, we get back to this truth: God has commanded us through Scripture to "go and make disciples." No matter our views, we must obey God's command.

We do not have to share our faith with our lips—our life is witness enough. Yes, the Bible teaches that our lifestyle should match with the Word. We preach by who we are. People learn about our faith by seeing us. As we have already discussed, lifestyle is a very important, powerful tool in evangelism.

However, the Bible also teaches that we are to open our mouth and share the Gospel: "So faith *comes* from hearing, and hearing by the word of Christ" (Romans 10:17). Those who have Christ must declare so. We must speak.

Discouragement.

We have already spoken of discouragement when studying perseverance. When discussing obstacles, it's necessary to revisit the subject and then move on.

During the years I have been in ministry, I have become convinced that the devil uses discouragement to arrest the Christian's progress. If we are discouraged, we will face difficulties in our own faith life, so naturally our ability to evangelize will also suffer. All who want to do the business of the Kingdom will encounter some form of attack that seeks to bring discouragement. When discouragement comes, courage goes. When courage goes, victory goes. Discouragement must be vanquished. Don't accept it; reject it firmly in the name of Jesus.

Sometimes we are discouraged by people we care about, sometimes by angry words or destructive criticism, sometimes through misunderstandings. These things happen to everyone, including Christians. Don't look to humans to ease your sorrow. Look to God. If someone has disappointed you, with God's help forgive them. Let it go!

At times we become disappointed because we are not seeing the results we want, when we want. This has caused some to quit. Sometimes success is instant, but too often people quit at the point they ought to begin. Remember this truth: "I will do what I can, and God will do what I can't."

What do Dr. Adonirum Judson, Hudson Taylor, and Dr. David Livingstone have in common? Two things: First, a great passion for lost souls which sent them to remote places; and second, perseverance. Seven years passed before Judson saw his first convert in Burma; it took Hudson Taylor seven years to see his first convert in China, and Livingstone waited seven years to see his first convert in Africa. Surely these men suffered discouragement, but they didn't allow it to stop God's work within them.

Don't allow discouragement to stop God's work within you. Bring it to Jesus; ask Him to strengthen you.

Satan.

Another hindrance to evangelism is Satan. When we set out to capture souls, we engage ourselves in conflict with the enemy of God, referred to in Scripture as the "tempter" (I Thessalonians 3:5), "accuser of our brethren" (Revelation 12:10), "father of lies" (John 8:44), "the ruler of the demons" (Matthew 12:24), "prince of the power of the air" (Ephesians 2:2), "angel of the abyss" (Revelation 9:11), "evil one" (Matthew 13:19), and "Your adversary" (I Peter 5:8).

In our cultured and "civilized" society, we have too often turned a blind eye to spiritual forces and assume they do not exist. Skeptics object to the existence of Satan; however, they cannot prove such non-existence. Some events are caused by natural laws, some by spiritual laws, and spiritual things cannot be proved by human means of knowing. We must accept the veracity of the Biblical accounts, and also the documented accounts past and present by both Christians and non-Christians who have been allowed in God's providence to see the spiritual forces. Not believing that the devil exists, as some people do, may give him some power or influence, because such people are ignorant of what the devil can do.

The Scriptures of both the Old and New Testaments tell us some of the works of the devil. From Genesis to Revelation, we are told of the devil tormenting people, possessing people, and afflicting people with infirmities and diseases. Some of the people possessed by demons became very violent and were easily recognizable as demon-possessed. But others looked so wholesome that no one could detect them without the gift of discernment of spirits. There is no reason to believe this has changed from Jesus' time to today. It is likely that we encounter demon oppressed or demon possessed individuals more often than we think.

Christians should understand the devil's malicious schemes and devices in order to combat him effectively. The devil is threatened when we launch evangelistic enterprises. He will try to do all that he can to stop them, by means of discouragement or whatever he sees to be a weakness. As the Apostle Peter warns, "Be of sober *spirit,* be on the alert. Your adversary, the devil, prowls around like a roaring lion, seeking someone to devour" (I Peter 5:8).

However, understanding the evil one does not imply fear. Christians must not fear the devil. God has all the power. Remember, "The Son of God appeared for this purpose, to destroy the works of the devil" (I John 3:8). The devil's power is restricted, and he will finally be confined to hell. That is the Good News!

In conclusion, obstacles will come in the way of the soul winner. While they are not pleasant, these obstacles can all be overcome because God is on our side. When we maintain a life of faith, prayer, and walking in the spirit daily, we will grow from strength to strength and win many souls for Christ.

Chapter 9
Objections

It would be convenient if the inquirer sat quietly, absorbed the message of salvation, and then accepted it instantly and without argument. This may indeed happen sometimes. However, it is likely that the inquirer will have some tough questions, and the soul winner must be prepared to answer. This chapter will deal with some of those questions.

I Believe That We Will All Be Saved (Universalist Position).

Universalists revere God's love. So do Christians, obviously—but we are not blinded by it. We know that God is not only loving but also just. We know that "the gate is small and the way is narrow that leads to life, and there are few who find it" (Matthew 7:14).

Universalism is a fully blown distortion of Scripture. It completely disregards the solid biblical teachings on salvation and hell.

Salvation. The Scriptures repeatedly teach that not all will receive eternal life, a fact ignored by universalists. Just a few examples: Pharoah's heart was hardened by God; Esau was rejected but Jacob chosen; the Chief Priests did not repent (Matthew 26). II Peter 3:7 says, "the present heavens and earth are being reserved for fire, kept for the day of judgment and destruction of ungodly men." This verse makes it clear that there are godly and ungodly people, and the fate of those two are not the same.

Retribution. Universalism is also inconsistent with the biblical doctrine of retribution. If all will be saved, why does the Bible repeatedly warn of the dangers of hell? If all will be saved, there is no reason for hell. And if there is no hell, what would people be saved *from?* Let's go back to Matthew 7:14 for a moment. Tucked at the end of that verse about the narrow way to life eternal is the phrase, *"and there are few who find it."* That doesn't sound like everyone's going to heaven, does it? We know from the Bible that God earnestly desires all to be saved: "God our Savior...desires all men to be saved and to come to the knowledge of the truth" (I Timothy 2:3-4). But not all accept His gift of life. The Bible teaches that the unsaved are destined for hell. Only those who turn to God in repentance and have faith in Lord Jesus will be saved.

On these grounds, we therefore must reject universalism and see it as part of the devil's strategy to deceive.

Which Religion Is The Correct One?

This is a question raised by people who are sincerely searching for truth, perhaps looking for a church that can help them.

Religion is us seeking God. This always fails. The *truth* is God is seeking us. He does this through the Person of the Lord Jesus Christ (John 1:17). Churches do not save; religions do not save; only Jesus saves. So the only correct answer to the question is to point to Jesus Christ, for salvation is only in the name of Jesus (John 14:6, Acts 4:12). You must challenge the inquirer to repent and seek Jesus, for He is the only Way.

Religion Is For The Weak.

I have rarely met people who are openly hostile to hearing the Gospel. However, during a visitation program in Scotland, I did encounter just such a person. A woman answered my knock at the door one day. When I told her that we were sharing the Good News of Jesus Christ, she shouted, "Religion is a crutch for the weak who fear hell!" and slammed the door in my face.

If you should meet such a person, point out how many great people of our day have believed in Jesus. Mention names of politicians, authors, other successful people, who have come to a saving faith. Our faith should not be dependent on other people, but this may help persuade some reluctant people that faith is not only for fearful people who want to escape; it is for everybody. In fact, it takes strength to be a believer.

God accepts young and old, shy and bold, weak and strong. God accepts you, and He will accept your inquirer.

I Tried It Before, But I Failed.

At times you will meet backslidden Christians who want to be restored back into fellowship with God. These Christians may feel fear or discouragement. To combat this, remind them to trust not in themselves but in Christ. Suggest to them that perhaps there had been one or two areas of their life which they hadn't yielded fully to Christ. Discuss this, being sure to provide comfort and strength, then lead them in a prayer of repentance and confession of their sins.

I Don't Believe In The Death Of Christ.

During my evangelistic career I have met some people who do not believe that Jesus died. However, even Muslims agree on the ascension of Christ. The Jewish secular historian Josephus, and other historians, refer to it. The death of Jesus is a well-documented fact that no intelligent person can deny.

I Do Not Believe In The Resurrection Of Christ.

Objections to Jesus' death and resurrection may be linked together, for some believe that He died but did not rise. For Christians, the death and the resurrection of Christ go hand-in-hand. The resurrection is the foundational truth to be received by all followers of Christ, making the death, burial, and resurrection of Christ the tenet of salvation. Thus, it is imperative that the inquirer, on the basis of the Word of God, accept it. The resurrection of Christ is well documented in Scripture. Christ rose from the dead. He was seen by Peter, He was seen by the disciples, He was seen and felt by Thomas, He was seen by more than 500 Christians at once, He was seen by Paul. To deny the resurrection of Christ is to deny the salvation He wrought.

Ask the inquirer to open up to the working of the Spirit. If they approach this truth with an open heart, God will tear the veil from the unbeliever's eyes and enable them to see the truth of our risen Lord.

If God Is A God Of Love, Why Is There So Much Suffering?

This is a common and understandable question. Often the inquirer is hurting due to past hardships or sufferings in his or her life, though sometimes the question is for the purpose of "catching" the soul winner. They may also ask, *Why are there so many wars? Why is there disease? Why are poor children dying of hunger?* These questions can become a stumbling block if the soul winner is not prepared to tackle them properly.

Answer the inquirer point blank, "God is love. His nature and character is love. But when God created humans, He gave them responsibility over the earth. Humans corrupted themselves, and sin entered the world. Wars and sufferings are caused by humanity."

The root of suffering is sin. The Bible says clearly that quarreling and wars have their origin in people (James 4:1-2). God has given humanity free will, and He holds humanity responsible for all its actions. Some people ask, *Why doesn't God stop all these things?* God has not stopped all these problems arising from our sin because He is giving us time to repent (Acts 17:30-31).

This objection must also be tackled by pointing to Jesus

71

as the great deliverer. As He delivered Israel because He saw that the Israelites were oppressed (Exodus 2:23-25), God always delivers the needy. Jesus called the oppressed and needy to come to Him, and was filled with compassion for them (Matthew 11:28); He declared that He had come to deliver them (Luke 4:18).

Throughout the discourse, keep pointing out to the inquirer that God wants to change *him* or *her*. Keep the focus. It's important that the person stops looking to past sufferings, afflictions, and other people; it's important that he or she stops blaming God, and instead looks to his or her own heart.

I Don't Believe In Life After Death.

This is an easy argument to deal with. You can use Biblical evidence; that is, if the inquirer believes that the Bible is the Word of God. The Bible clearly teaches that there is life after death (John 5:24, John 11:24-26, Romans 5:17). There will be a resurrection of the just and the unjust: the just unto everlasting life, the unjust unto everlasting destruction (Revelation 20:12-14, 21:8). If the inquirer does not accept the Bible as the Word of God, you can use historical evidence. People of all walks of life have always believed in life after death, seeing the end of life not as the end but as the beginning. It's necessary to believe in life after death, because the decisions we make now determine where we will spend eternity.

Tackling Objections.

The objections we have covered above, and how you can tackle them, prepare you to be more effective. New objections will arise, and you will need to develop skills to tackle them as well. Tackling objections requires sensitivity and, above all else, prayer. Some of the objectors have satisfactorily evolved advanced arguments in favor of their position. If you are not strong in your own faith and very familiar with

God's Word, you will be unable to be persuasive.

When dealing with the objectors, prayer is the key that will open their hearts. In presenting the strategies, I do not underestimate the power of God speaking through you in His infinite wisdom and enabling you to use words beyond human wisdom, and win the objector. And yes, the Holy Spirit will give us the words to say, but remember—"knowledge is power."

So know your Bible. The Holy Scriptures emphatically declare in II Timothy 2:15: "Be diligent to present yourself approved to God as a workman who does not need to be ashamed, accurately handling the word of truth." While secular education brings with it respect, knowledge, world applause, and human philosophy, Biblical education brings credibility, godly approval, and effectiveness in evangelism.

Handling objections will lead the objector to a saving knowledge of Jesus Christ and will also broaden your understanding and further enhance your evangelistic ministry.

Chapter 10

Healings and Other Miracles

The subject of miracles stimulates interest in some Christians but raises suspicion in others. Those who hold a negative view have undoubtedly come across a false witness who claimed to have healing powers or to have experienced a special miracle in order to gratify his or her own ego or to gain publicity. Nevertheless, we must discuss miracles. A consideration of dynamic evangelism would not be complete or balanced without mention of this important subject.

Before we can proceed further, I would like to state that *everything* in Christianity is a miracle. All the great Christian truths—salvation, the Incarnation, the virgin birth, the resurrection—are all miracles. Everything God does is a miracle. The Bible is a book of miracles from beginning to end.

"I am the first and the last, and the living One; and I was dead, and behold, I am alive forevermore" (Revelation 1:17-18). Christians believe the resurrection of Jesus was the greatest of all miracles. This was *the resurrection*, our hope for eternal life, proof that God will raise all those who have died in Christ. Indeed, God's power in Christ at the resurrection caused many saints who had died also to be resurrected, and they were seen walking in the streets of Jerusalem (Matthew 27:52-53).

Before we move on to the subject of healings, let us consider the broader topic of miracles in general. Correct understanding of miracles is necessary, but the fact is that they are a great mystery. Though we can all attest to them, we have difficulty defining them, for we are ordinary, and miracles are extraordinary.

So what is a miracle? A miracle is when God sovereignly intervenes and makes manifest His omnipotent power by mighty acts that are out of the realms of the natural. Almost all miracles involve a deviation from the usual operations of natural laws. Although all God's miracles have tangible valid proof of their occurrence, it's not always the kind of "proof" that some insist upon as clear evidence. The real issue with those who do not believe is that they lack proper Biblical faith. One who has real faith believes that God can do anything He wills, including miracles far beyond our comprehension, whether we actually see them happening or not. God can and will perform miracles in the sovereignty of His will, and in accordance with His plans and purposes.

That said, only credible miracles bring credibility to the message, and the messenger must be one who truly possesses the gifts of the working of miracles. I must restate the fact that we need *credible* miracles, because where the veracity and integrity of miracles are in question, the hearts of the regenerate have been hardened. *Truthfulness* determines the authenticity of miracles. Unfortunately, this is often not the case. False claims of miracles have always brought bankruptcy and discrepancy to the message: "in their greed they will exploit you with false words" (II Peter 2:3). Due to too many of these false teachers and also our lack of documentation of genuine miracles, a lot of people in the world are now very skeptical. *The church must gain credibility in this area.*

Christians should be bothered by the absence of miracles. We must yearn for miracles in our generation and ask, as Gideon did, "where are all His miracles which our fathers told us about, saying, 'Did not the LORD bring us up from

75

Egypt?'" (Judges 6:13). Why do we need miracles today? By way of answer, let us establish the real purpose of miracles.

Miracles Glorify God.

After Jesus healed the man born blind in John 9:3, He explained to those gathered around that "it was so that the works of God might be displayed in him." Similarly, when Jesus heard that His dear friend Lazarus was near death, He said, "This sickness is not to end in death, but for the glory of God, so that the Son of God may be glorified by it" (John 11:4). Thus, if miracles display the glory of God, then the absence of miracles should not be accepted as the norm.

Miracles Display The Love And Grace Of God.

Another reason Jesus performed healing miracles was that He had compassion. (Matthew 14:14). The heart of Jesus went out to people in their needs and distresses (Luke 7:13). He raised the widow's son at Nain because He cared for her, as the young man was her only son. The healing of the man at the pool of Bethesda is a great demonstration of the grace of God in working miracles in His sovereign will and time (John 5). Miracles declare the love, compassion, and grace of God. The church must ask for more miracles.

Miracles Demonstrate The Power Of God.

God gives His people power to perform miracles, for miracles attest His power. There are many such acts recorded in the Bible. In John 11, Lazarus had died. This was not in doubt: everybody who knew Lazarus knew that he had died. He had been in the grave for four days. Mourners were still gathered. But Jesus came and raised him back to life. So strong was the power of the miracle that "many of the Jews who...saw what He had done, believed in Him" (John 11:45). The Pharisees and Chief Priests also reacted strongly to this power: "What are we doing? For this man is performing many signs. If we let Him go on like this, all men will believe in Him, and the Romans will come and take away both our place and our nation" (John 11:47-48).

Miracles Cause People To Believe The Gospel.

We saw above that those who saw Lazarus raised from the dead put their faith in Jesus. The Scriptures vividly teach similar coming to faith elsewhere: Acts 8:6-8, Acts 9:35,42, John 2:11, and Exodus 4:8, among many others. We are encouraged to know that the Scriptures endorse miracles and that people believe because of them.

Miracles Demonstrate That The Kingdom Of God Is Both Present And Future.

Miracles declare Christ's Kingdom. Jesus declared, "But if I cast out demons by the Spirit of God, then the kingdom of God has come upon you" (Matthew 12:28). We must proclaim the Gospel, and, as we are told in Matthew 10:7-9: "And as you go, preach, saying, 'The kingdom of heaven is at hand.' Heal *the* sick, raise *the* dead, cleanse *the* lepers, cast out demons. Freely you received, freely give" (Matthew 10:7-9). See also Luke 9:1-2, Matthew 4:23; 9:35, Acts 8:13 and Mark 16:15-18.

Healings.

Dynamic evangelism is evident in miracles and healings. Healings have always had an important place in the Christian faith, though in some times and places more than others. As we look at the life of the church in general, we see that healings are happening in many churches, across denominational boundaries. The healings that are happening today are only a foretaste of what God wants to do. There are many people that are in need of divine healing.

It's fair to say that all Christians believe in divine healings, although Christians differ in their beliefs and practices. Some exercise healing gifts by the laying on of hands as commanded by Jesus in Mark 16:18, by anointing with oil as expressed in James 5:14, and by offering prayers of faith (James 5:15-16). Among those who do not exercise healing gifts, there are usually prayers offered on behalf of the sick.

This leads us to an important point: the standard Pentecostal doctrine on healing has always been "there is healing provided for in the atonement." This implies that all Christians can experience physical healing, as it was already provided for in the atonement. This is supported by citing verses such as Isaiah 53:5, 1 Peter 2:24-25. Historically this doctrine has often been condemned as heretical by some Calvinists, who argue that the verses used by Pentecostals in favor of their doctrine have been misinterpreted and misunderstood. Calvinists also point out the fact that Christians have always been sick, age and eventually die, and argue that it's not therefore possible for healing to have been provided for in the atonement.

The crucial question is, as always, "What do the Scriptures say?" We must always look to the Bible, because opinions of theologians and commentators differ. It has all the answers and is the absolute authority. So what does the Bible actually teach about healing?

For our answer it's worth examining the healing ministry of Jesus. The Gospel writers portray the Lord's healing miracles as the focus of His ministry. The Gospel according to Luke is a particularly intriguing one, as he examines the healing miracles from a general practitioner's perspective. He gives us clear and vivid depictions of the background and symptoms of the diseases, a diagnosis, and a cure.

There is no reason to believe the healing miracles of our Lord ended with the Gospels. Indeed, it seems clear that the Lord continued performing His healing ministry in the book of Acts, through His disciples. The ministry of Jesus was attested to by many great healings; this is why evangelism is to be accompanied by physical healings. As John Wesley said, "If God can save the soul, He can heal the body also." This healing power still exists in the present church.

Why is it necessary for healings to go hand in hand in evangelism? After all, the primary task of the evangelist is to lead people to salvation (Romans 1:16). Maybe Dr. Schofield's definition of salvation, which he gives in his reference Bible comment on Romans 1:16, provides the link: "healing, deliverance, wholeness, prosperity and soundness." The unregenerate are in need of salvation, and healing is included in the act of salvation, though the extent and expanse of that healing may not be instantly felt. There is a divine act of healing that is subsequent to conversion, and that healing may not necessarily be physical healing. All are in need of some manner of healing. Healing and wholeness come as part and parcel of salvation.

In answering why healing must accompany evangelism, we can see that healing meets many of the definitions of a miracle as set out earlier in this chapter.

Healings Demonstrate The Love And Grace Of God. Matthew 8:16 says, "When evening came, they brought to Him many who were demon-possessed; and He cast out the spirits with a word, and healed all who were ill." Note that Jesus healed all the sick. Nowhere in Scripture do we see the Lord turning away anyone who truly sought him in faith. All who went to Him received healing. Also, His compassion is referred to many times in the Gospels. There are many accounts of Jesus being filled with compassion and cleansing lepers, bringing sight to the blind, healing the sick, and much more. We believe God's grace and compassion are with us today, thus we believe that there is always God's potential to heal all the sick for whom we pray.

Healings Demonstrate The Power Of God. Healings demonstrate the power of God to the Christian and non-Christian alike. Jesus healed *all manner* of afflictions. No sickness, disease, or demon possession could withstand Him. We know His fame grew because of the healings and miracles He performed;

people knew who He was because they saw His miracles. It's one thing to preach that God will heal the sick, and quite another to actually see the sick being healed. Many people from all walks of life have come to saving faith in Christ because of healing miracles.

Healings Cause People To Believe In The Gospel. I once preached in a Muslim village where there was an 18-year-old blind girl. As the people listened attentively, we prayed for her in simple faith…and she opened her eyes and began to see. This single miracle sparked the flames for revival in that village, and many Muslims who had been hostile toward the Gospel became receptive. Many people are attracted to Gospel crusades because they need physical healing; many people have been saved because they or someone they knew got healed. Healing can be a valuable witness.

Healings Demonstrate That The Kingdom Of God Is Both Present And Future. Healings, like all miracles, declare that the Kingdom of God is now and here. Jesus, the King of the Kingdom, banishes sickness and disease, and the sick are healed in His Name. In Luke 10:9 Jesus instructs His followers: "Whatever city you enter and they receive you, eat what is set before you; and heal those in it who are sick, and say to them, 'The kingdom of God has come near to you.'" This is why the disciples "*began* going throughout the villages, preaching the gospel and healing everywhere" (Luke 9:6).

A question that troubles many people is, "Why do some people get healed and others not?" We must deal with this question. The truth is, there are many people we pray for who will not be healed the way they want to be. Some become embittered by the situation and not bettered. For those people, the question is always "Why me?"

To answer this briefly, let me state that just because the healing hasn't occurred yet does not mean that it won't happen. *Delays* are not *denials*. Additionally, healing may have taken place, just not in the manner the sufferer had asked for. People always look for physical healing, but God may heal the invisible but greater spiritual and emotional maladies. Since healing is an act of God, He alone determines how to dispense it, on whom, and when. We must let God be God. He works in His own way and time according to His sovereign counsel.

Other blocks to healing include unforgiveness and bitterness (James 5:14-15, Mark 2:5, II Chronicles 7:14), and lack of faith (Mark 6:4-6). When Jesus healed people, He often commended them for their faith, implying or even saying outright that it's their faith that made their healing possible for them (Mark 5:34, 10:52; Matthew 9:22, 8:32, 9:29, 15:28; Luke 17:19, 18:42).

Although normally faith precedes healing, there are times when God, in His infinite wisdom and love, does heal people without their possessing any faith in Him. Often, these people come to faith upon having received their healing miracle. This is now happening in places where the Gospel has not yet penetrated.

I have been involved in the healing ministry for over a decade. If someone were to ask me for an explanation why some people get healed and not others, I would answer as above, but also add without any reservation: Christianity is a mystery, miracles are a mystery and so are healings. Therefore, I cannot fully explain why some people get healed and not others. It's God's act.

The other question that is usually asked in Christian circles is, "Is it God's will *always* to heal?" Some have the opinion that sometimes it's God's will for some to be healed, others not; others are of the opinion that it's always God's will to heal.

If we accept that it is always God's will to heal, then why aren't we all healed? If we believe that it's not always God's will to heal, then why bother to pray for the sick? Further, how do we distinguish those who are to be healed from those who are not? This can sound like the question of evangelizing to the elect. Those who teach that it is not always God's will to heal insist that we must pray and discern whether it's God's will to heal in every affliction. I agree. This is because the greatest blessing for a Christian is finding out God's will and hearing His voice in every situation.

But this raises the uncomfortable question, "Is it God's will for someone to be sick?" Some say yes, adding that God teaches us lessons through sickness; they prove this view by citing Timothy, who had an incurable stomach problem, and Paul with his thorn in the flesh. Others say no, and point out that sickness does not glorify God; they prove their point by quoting Galatians 3:13 (the curse of sickness has been removed), and Isaiah 53:4 and I Peter 2:23-24 (Christ healed all).

What is my answer? The Kingdom has come—but not in its fullness. We're caught between the "now" and the "not yet." We can clearly assert that God is always willing to heal, but that although He has the power to heal all, not all will be healed. This runs parallel to the fact that while God's desire is for all to be saved, not all will be saved.

Since evangelists are entrusted with the Gospel of life, they must minister in the power of the Spirit and ensure that people are healed spiritually and emotionally, as well as physically. They must minister the full Gospel to the whole person, which will touch and bring healing to the body, soul, and spirit.

What can we do to create the atmosphere for healings? There are certain things we can do to create that atmosphere, and there are certain things that only Almighty God can do. God will do His part, but for us to move on from a people that preaches about healings to a people that operates in the gifts of healings, we must fulfill certain conditions.

We Must Ask For Healings For The Right Reasons And Not For The Wrong Ones. Though God will grant healings according to His perfect will even when motives are questionable, it is absolutely necessary for a child of God to ask for healings with proper motives. Some people ask for healings for all sorts of reasons, and wrong motives, such as to gain publicity, may stop God from performing the healing miracle. When the Pharisees and Sadducees asked Jesus for a sign from heaven for wrong reasons, He refused (Matthew 16:1-3).

We Must Become Strong In Faith. The doubting, uncertain Christian is a great hindrance to healings. The church is sometimes powerless to bring healing, because many in her midst lack proper Biblical faith for the miraculous. Jesus once admonished the disciples, who were frustrated over their inability to heal. To their questions of why they were so powerless in this situation, Jesus replied, "because of the littleness of your faith..." (Matthew 17:14-22). God requires Christians to exercise faith for healings. There are probably some situations where you felt powerless. You need faith so that nothing becomes impossible for you. This is the message that should be inscribed upon every church: "Have faith in God" (Matthew 21:21, Mark 9:23, 11:22-24, Hebrews 11:1-6, Romans 4:16-25, James 5:15).

We Must Fast. Matthew 17:21 says, "But this kind does not go out except by prayer and fasting." Though some Bible translations omit verse 21, I have quoted it because it presents to us the absolute necessity of fasting. It's thought-provoking to see how prayer is linked to fasting; and it's recommended that you add fasting to your prayer life to give prayer a dynamic power to release healings and miracles.

We Must Publicly And Privately Exalt The Name Of Jesus Christ. We must have Him as the central theme of our message—not healings, miracles, or anything else. True preaching honors and exalts the name of Jesus. Healing is only obtainable through His Name (Acts 4:30, 3:6, 3:16, 4:10).

We Must Overcome Our Fears. When we do so, we will lay our hands on the sick as the Lord commanded (Mark 16:18), anoint them with oil in the name of the Lord (James 5:14), and trust God's Spirit within us to minister healing using methods that He alone wants.

Miracles are not only a part of church history; they also play an important role in our modern church. Pessimists would have us believe that there will only be counterfeit miracles in our day. True, there are counterfeit miracles— but we are to praise God for the many true miracles He performs. Cessationists argue that the whole theology of miracles is built entirely from the book of Acts, and that it is a transitional book, solely from which one cannot build a doctrine. To this we reply; Acts *is* a transitional book, but the acts of the Holy Spirit were meant to be demonstrated in the churches until the Lord returns. Miracles should be the norm in every church. In fact, we should be surprised if miracles are *not* happening. Miracles have always been happening, and historical findings prove miracles throughout church history.

Step out in faith and let the sick be healed, to bring glory to God!

Chapter 11

Deliverance

"When Jesus had called the Twelve together, he gave them power and authority to drive out all demons and to cure diseases..." (Luke 9:1).

In our consideration of evangelism, I have postponed until now the important issue of deliverance. The subject cannot be thoroughly covered without taking a survey of the teachings of the Scriptures, both Old Testament and New, as well as considering the deliverance ministry as practiced by our Lord and in the early church. This teaching must be carried out by someone who has made deliverance ministry both a specialty and a practice. Therefore, knowing that I have no such complete and full qualifications for this great work, I will confine myself to the scriptural teachings and add a little insight from my experience.

What has the study of demons to do with evangelism? Everything. Evangelism that does not deliver people from every work and scheme of Satan does not have the desired end result. The Lord Himself spent a lot of time in the deliverance ministry, and evangelism that ministers full deliverance is still necessary today. Studying this question will further strengthen your evangelistic calling and gifts, enabling you to use the authority and power that is invested in the name of Jesus Christ to cast out demons.

Jesus launched the deliverance ministry and continued to

minister deliverance through His disciples (Matthew 10:1). The Scriptures teach that Jesus sent out the seventy in teams of two (Luke 10:1, 17) on what seemed to be impossible missions. However, those seventy men exercised power over the devils so that when their preaching tour came to its consummation, they "returned with joy, saying, 'Lord, even the demons are subject to us in Your name'" (Luke 10:17). This ought to be a normal occurrence in everyday evangelism.

Demons do exist and there are many people troubled by them, in all societies and cultures. The Scriptures nowhere teach that the activities of Satan or his demons have changed.

A worthy evangelistic ministry must study deliverance from a biblical perspective so as to be able to minister to all people, especially those under the domain of darkness. We should contemplate all that Jesus did: exercised unlimited power and authority over Satan and demons, gave His own disciples power and authority over all the demonic forces, continued to minister deliverance through the early church, and enabled the church today to deliver people from demonic oppressions and possessions.

Study in evangelistic theology should not be limited to deliverance from demons, although that is an integral ministry in power evangelism. There is a neglect of teaching in the areas of satanology and demonology on the part of some theologians, aside from a limited survey of the origin of Satan and his fall, and perhaps a passing reference to demons as portrayed in the Gospels. Theological writers in some instances have had a lack of preparation to deal with deliverance. One theologian, in his volume of systematic theology, often uses the phrase, "the devil once was...." It's not surprising that any theologian, scholar, clergyman or layman who considers the devil as a being that "once was" may not be inclined to see the devil's current activities, and the subject of deliverance will be deemed unnecessary.

One of the major works of Satan is to seek to hinder people from accepting the Lord Jesus Christ. We also know that Satan is the ruler of demons, but now we will study one of the most fascinating mysteries of Christianity: every believer has been given power over all the power of the enemy (Mark 16:15-20). Jesus assures us, "I have given you authority to tread on serpents and scorpions, and over all the power of the enemy, and nothing will injure you" (Luke 10:19). This is why the spirits were subject to the disciples in Jesus' name.

I will now state two important principles on demonology. First, the Bible warns us not to be ignorant about the devil, and that we must "be of sober spirit, be on the alert. Your adversary, the devil, prowls around like a roaring lion, seeking someone to devour" (1 Peter 5:8). Therefore it's utter folly for a church to omit this all-important subject. Second, while not omitting it, we must not over-teach on this subject. There are some who teach on the devil and demons with far more longevity than does the Bible. This type of teaching empowers the devil and discredits God.

The correct teaching on the knowledge, power, work, and activities of the devil and demons must be properly and scripturally balanced by stating the omnipotence of our God and also by reaffirming the fact that Jesus has given the believer power and authority over all devils and all demons. It is comforting to note that no Christian need fear the devil, for on the final day we will look at him and say to him, "Is this the man who made the earth tremble, who shook kingdoms, who made the world like a wilderness and overthrew its cities, who did not allow his prisoners to go home?" (Isaiah 14:16-17).

This is important. An overemphasis of teaching about demons has brought disastrous results in some churches where some people are seeing demons all over the place and attempting to deliver people who are mentally retarded and not in any way demon possessed.

However, deliverance must be given its proper place in evangelism, because there are many people in dire need of deliverance. After all, we have already seen that the definition of "salvation" includes deliverance. Christians will not be able to deliver people from the kingdom of darkness into the Kingdom of God until they first take their God-given authority over Satan and all his works.

In Chapter 8 we touched on the subject of Satan, his other names, his powers, and his limitations. We know that Satan seeks to destroy people without cause (Job 1:12, John 10:10), that he torments, kills, steals, and imposes fear on people. It is important to reiterate that though the devil has power, he is not all-powerful. Though he knows some things, he is not all-knowing. God alone is all-powerful and all-knowing. We will briefly mention some of the activities of Satan which we did not cover previously, then we will show you that as a believer you have power to minister deliverance to all who have been made captive by Satan.

Where Did The Devil Come From?

The Scriptures do not give us every detail regarding the career and occupation of the devil in eternity past, but we are provided with considerable information on his personality, work, and activities. The teaching in the Scriptures is sufficient and complete, and as such we do not require further knowledge on this subject, other than that which is written. From Scripture we gather that Satan was created with "the seal of perfection, full of wisdom and perfect in beauty" (Ezekiel 28:12). He once was the anointed guardian cherub on God's holy mountain (Ezekiel 28:14). (In the Scriptures, cherubim and seraphim guard the throne of God, and as such they are ever in His presence.) Many feel that the implication of being on God's holy mountain is that Satan worshipped God. Although

Satan was created in a state of perfect beauty, he did not keep his estate, and fell into sin. The wickedness that was found in him (Ezekiel 28:15) is thought to be attempting to usurp God's throne. Thus, the principal cause of Satan's downfall is that of pride.

It's commonly believed that God cast out Satan from his first estate, since sin cannot dwell in the presence of a holy God. This brings up a question: "Since God in His foreknowledge knew that Satan would attempt to dethrone Him and cause angels and man to sin, why did He create him?" This is a difficult question to which I cannot give a full answer, but I can give a partial one: if Satan had not sinned, then there would have been no sin at all. If there were no sin, Adam would not have sinned, and God's redemption plan through the sacrifice of Jesus Christ would not have been achieved.

Can Satan Be Present Everywhere At The Same Time? Does He Possess People?

The answer to the first question is no. God alone is omnipresent. Satan can only be in one place at one time. As for the second question, it seems that on rare occasions, Satan himself took possession of people. Note the strange activity of Satan in Acts 5:3, where it mentions that Satan filled the heart of Ananaias and Sapphira, and in John 13:27, where Satan enters Judas. He may do the same again today; the Scriptures do not say otherwise.

Satan likes to "sift" Christians "like wheat," as he desired to do with Peter, perhaps an allusion to a strategy of weakening or damaging the believer's faith by planting seeds of doubt which cause them to fall into Satan's hands. There are many Christians being sifted today, but those who remain firmly grounded in God's Word will be safe. They will remain strong and victorious through the sifting process that comes upon them, and they will strengthen fellow believers.

Who And What Are Demons?

This is where we start in deliverance ministry. Demons are Satan's agents, unclean spirits whose activities are limited, but they nonetheless have some power. They seem to have fallen after Satan's downfall, when he successfully used his powers of seduction and deception in the heavenly realms and caused a third of the angels to join him in his rebellion against God. The Scriptures refer to them as the "angels [who] sinned" (2 Peter 2:4) and "angels who did not keep their own domain, but abandoned their proper abode" (Jude 6). The reference in Matthew 25:41 to "the devil and his angels" seems to indicate Satan's full control over the angels who joined his alliance in his attempt to topple God. It seems likely that the biblical references to demons, unclean spirits, and evil spirits refer to those fallen angels.

Demons are spiritual beings, and as such, they may not be visible to human eyes, although there have been many reliable accounts of people seeing demons. In general, since demons are spirits and do not have bodies, they must be seen through the eyes of discernment. The New Testament often mentions demons and unclean spirits. Jesus frequently rebuked and cast out evil spirits from people, and taught His disciples how to exercise power over them. It is apparent that demonic activities still exist, and the church must continue doing the works that Jesus did, and continue to manifest the presence of His Kingdom by casting out evil spirits. An understanding of the devil and demons will prepare you so you can confront and drive out devils.

Are Satan And His Demons Responsible For All The Bad Things That Happen?

Satan can inflict some sicknesses, but not all sicknesses are from him (Job 2:7 and Luke 13:11-16). Demons cause some people dumbness (Luke 11:14, Matthew 9:32) but at times can also speak through people (Matthew 16:21-23).

The Scriptures seem to indicate that demon possessions can at times cause violent actions (Luke 8:26-29) and even the appearance of a mental disorder (John 10:20). The Gospels present many incidences of people who were possessed by demons. Some of them looked so nice that it was not possible to detect with the natural eye that they were demonized (Luke 4:13), while others were extreme cases of possession, such as in Mark 5:1-17.

Demons seek to cause rebellion against God (Rev 16:14), and some influence of demonization can be seen in the superhuman strength in some of those who are possessed (Mark 5:1-5). Some of the mysterious catastrophes, chaos, accidents, and events that occur today are almost certainly his work. We know from the Bible that he is capable of causing fire to fall from heaven (Job 1:16), and hurricanes (Job 1:19). But having said that, we must remember that Satan can do nothing outside of God's permissive will. After all, all the sufferings that were inflicted on Job were allowed by God (Job 1:12, 2:3).

Though Satan is not all-powerful, as we have said, people still need deliverance from Satan's influence and evil-doing. People in need of deliverance may include those involved in witchcraft or who have been to a witch or witchdoctor, clairvoyant, tarot card reader, or astrologer; those who practice divination or use Ouija boards; those involved in the martial arts; and those involved in the occult or in groups such as Hare Krishna, Spiritualists, Transcendental Meditation, New Age, or many others. Those who have been exposed to pornographic literature also need deliverance, as they do from uncleanness, wickedness, violence, fear, and curses.

We must be a people that will walk by faith bringing deliverance to the captives. When you spend time with God in prayer and fasting, you will gain anointing, power, and holiness, which will cause demons to flee away. Without the strength born of prayer and fasting, some demon activities will not be restricted as they should be in the name of Jesus. Deliverance ministry is now made possible through the Word. Study the Word, live the Word, and quote the Word as Jesus did, even in the hour of His temptation.

Lastly, recognize the power that is in the name and also the blood of Jesus and apply it in faith. Loudly call upon the Name of Jesus for your strength and you will be used of God for the ministry of deliverance.

Chapter 12
Methods of Evangelism

Methods are but a means to an end. Some which were successful years ago may not be successful today. Some work as well today as they did two hundred years ago. Some have yet to be explored. Growing evangelistic churches are adding new methods to the old, tried-and-true methods.

There are a variety of methods that can be considered. Since we are not able to cover every one, we'll consider just some that are most prevalent.

Gospel Crusades.

Crusade evangelization is one of the most popular methods currently used. Dr. Billy Graham comes to nearly everyone's mind when they think about crusades, though of course there are many other crusaders.

A crusade means a gathering together for a common goal. Historically, the word has been used to refer to military battles for occupation, invasion, and possession of lands. It was also used in the historic crusades of Europe, the great battles fought by Constantine, Charlemagne and others. The Church of Rome employed the term to wage war for possession of the Holy Land from Islam. There is some debate on the use of the term in modern evangelism, because of some of its negative connotations. However, I am convinced that the use of the term in evangelism is consistent with its task. Since early in this book we established that soul winning is akin to a military exercise, what better term could be used?

93

Many evangelists yearn to lead crusades, for there is such exuberant joy at these events: singing, preaching, and altar calls. There is indeed a need for new crusaders, as the veteran crusaders may soon be finishing their work. The question many novice crusaders ask is, "How can I conduct a large scale crusade?"

If you want to be used in great gospel crusades, you must first have the call from God. Second, learn from current successful crusaders. Third, go and do! In addition to that, you must plan: lay out strategies, enlist prayers, financial support, technical support, and personnel; train counselors, choose a great venue accessible by all; arrange transport; organize publicity and discipleship programs; and set up a crusade board.

Some Christians are against gospel crusades. Some arguments against crusades are as follows:

• Mass evangelism leads to ecumenism, and some believe ecumenism to be unscriptural.

• Statistics show that most people who make decisions at mass crusades drift away; therefore, these crusades do not produce many genuine conversions.

• Crusades require people to make decisions, and Christ commanded us to make *disciples* not *decision-makers*.

• Crusades are exorbitant to run, and Christians must be good stewards of resources.

• Follow-up work must be done, or the crusade will fail.

• Most mass crusades are centered around one great evangelist, and Christ's command is for us to teach those who can teach others.

We must study these arguments and bring about radical changes to prevent failure in evangelism. An evangelist who does not look at the pros and cons of mass evangelism is short-sighted.

There are also advantages to crusades:
- Crusades can lead people to actual repentance and faith and have been used of God for the conversion of many people
- Often held at stadiums, parks, tents, and fields, which venues have been pivotal in attracting crowds of all sorts, crusades provide a neutral ground for people who fear entering a church.
- Crusades promote a measure of unity in the churches in the towns where they are held.
- Crusades can provide good fellowship for Christians who might not usually meet together.
- A crowd always attracts a crowd. Crusades impact whole cities, as big numbers always catch attention of the media, politicians, and people from all walks of life and cultures.

Personal Evangelism.

Person-to-person evangelism is largely what has been discussed up to now in this book. It is one of the most successful methods of evangelism and is greatly honored by God. It's been established that it produces great results and real disciples. The greatest strength of personal evangelism lies in the fact that it uses the gifts of every Christian; every Christian can and must be involved. The fastest-growing churches in Latin America, Africa, and North America have seen great results through "contagious" Christian living, or every Christian becoming contagious and infectious in sharing their faith. If the lost art of disciple-making were restored, and every Christian witnessed vigorously and devotedly, the whole world could be evangelized very quickly.

The flexibility of personal evangelism is thrilling: you can do it anywhere, with everyone, and anytime. Personal evangelism has always been very effective, so we must continue using it. All personal workers who engage in evangelism daily, diligently, and devotedly will win many souls. Their work culminates in true biblical discipleship.

Door-To-Door Evangelism.

Nowadays in western countries, not so many individuals and churches are engaged in door-to-door evangelism. It's considered uncultured, an invasion of privacy; people are afraid of being branded "religious lunatics." I have asked many Christians whether they engage in this method of evangelism, and often the answer is, "No, Brother Luke! People will think we're Jehovah's Witnesses!"

The conclusion I reach is that these Christians are afraid of other people's opinions. Sure, the Jehovah's Witnesses are doing it; they have become renowned for this. And you know what? It's working for them. Door to door evangelism *works* when the approach is good. It is recommended that we always go two by two, as Jesus sent out the seventy in twos.

Many people will open their hearts if only you visit them. You will meet isolated people, depressed, suicidal, and bored people, sick people, and people with a variety of needs, all waiting to hear the Good News. Wake up, church. Knock on doors!

Tract Distribution.

It's always a good time to sow Gospel seeds. While with tract distribution we may not actually see the fruit in this life, it's our responsibility to sow seeds and God's responsibility to save. We must constantly trust God to accomplish the desired results.

Tract distribution is an exciting and very easy ministry to carry out. There are many places we can distribute materials: shopping malls, street corners, parks, hospitals, prisons, anywhere people are found. Giving out tracts in the streets also opens up conversation for the personal worker. It's a wonderful ministry for churches to give tracts to every household in the community. Ideally, the tract should have a contact phone number in case the inquirer wants to pursue the matter further.

Servant Evangelism.

Servant evangelism is a very effective form of evangelism. This is a good method for those who have been fearful to evangelize in other, more vocal ways. It's very effective because Christians go into the community and serve people, sharing God's love.

In servant evangelism, Christians identify the needs in the community and then go out and put their faith into actions. There are unlimited projects you can do: feed hungry people, serve coffee in the streets, meals on wheels, mow lawns, give away soda or lemonade on a hot day, hold free car washes, and any other practical work that you can do for someone in Jesus' name. This will really touch the unregenerate and cause them to think.

Servant evangelism touches many people the church has been unable to touch, especially those who are biased against the church, who perhaps feel the church wants to get something out of them. No amount of words can change such thinking—but this mentality can be penetrated by servant evangelism. Servant evangelism paves the way for personal evangelism. It's a heart opener.

Friendship Evangelism.

This means the attempt by a Christian to lead someone to a saving knowledge of Jesus Christ as Lord and Savior through their friendship. A Christian who embarks on friendship evangelism must do so under all circumstances and at all times.

This is a proven method of evangelizing people in religious groups and the unchurched devoid of Christian love in Jesus. In friendship evangelism, you become a friend to the unconverted. You sow love. You help them out. You stand with them in adversity. You do all that a good friend can do.

Many societies are no longer community-based. Many people are lonely, isolated, longing for real friendships. This is why the church is presented with such an enormous task to share the Gospel in a friendly manner. Conversions have often been through personal contacts, and almost always a gradual process rather than an instant decision.

When friendship has done its work, the unregenerate will ask, "Why are you doing all this for me?" It may take weeks, months, or years before they reach this point, but they will reach it. When they ask this all-important question, it's the right time to preach to them of Jesus and Him crucified.

March For Jesus.

Since "March for Jesus" was launched in the United Kingdom, a number of cities in the U.K and other cities in many nations have experienced their own version of "March for Jesus." Unbelievers begin to ask questions when they see Christians marching in the streets, smiling, singing, lifting up the banner of Jesus. The "March for Jesus" rallies have produced some good results, and they play an important role in the churches that participate and in the cities where they are held.

Open-Air Campaigns.

Open-air campaigns are popular in Africa and other countries. These are small meetings that can be conducted by a few people. They are cost-effective and provide good opportunities for people to hear the Gospel in the streets, villages, and town squares. They are similar to crusades, except that they are conducted in the open and do not usually attract large crowds. This, however, is changing, with an increasing hunger for the Gospel. It's great to see young people conducting open-air campaigns, which provide good platforms for future great evangelists. God has used open-air campaigns in big ways.

Social Work Evangelism.

Many churches are involved in social work today. Due to the many needs that arise in society, such as unemployment, homelessness, bereavement, depression, prostitution, and drug addiction, churches must work to reach these people through social work. However, good churches must do social *work* but shun the social *gospel*. Social work glorifies God when the Gospel of Jesus Christ is preached and sinners converted. If this is lacking, the church becomes only a club doing good deeds.

Food Parcels.

Numerous churches are becoming increasingly aware of meeting the needs in their communities. This has caused them to sense the need for taking food parcels to needy families. This presents the church a chance to do the works of Jesus. Sometimes people do not just need the words but the compassion of Christ.

Radio And T.V. Evangelism.

We live in an era when radio and television are important tools of communication. There are unprecedented and unparalleled opportunities today to preach on the radio and television. Many evangelists are now on the air. At this point in time, America leads the world in T.V evangelism. Radio and television ministries are mushrooming not only in the U.S., but worldwide. Even in Muslim countries, such as in the Middle East and North Africa, and in other countries where preaching the Gospel is not permitted, the Gospel can still be aired to those countries via such media as radio, television, internet, satellite, and no doubt by as yet unconceived means. It's wonderful that today the Gospel can be preached to the "closed" countries in such diverse ways. This makes the so-called "closed" countries open! Now is the time for evangelists and pastors to preach on radio and television in their own language and cultural identity. The need today in developing countries is to train their own nationals who are better equipped to reach their own people than are foreigners. Though missionaries are still needed worldwide, most missiologists agree that supporting local workers in their native lands is cheaper and more effective than sending missionaries. In all these, there needs to be a proper balance. Christians need to participate fully in radio, television, and all forms of media to spread the Gospel.

The Internet.

As the Internet continues to expand, it is a unique moment for some evangelists to tap in and use it rightfully. The whole world is at your fingertips via the Internet, which can be used as a good tool for evangelism today.

Prayer.

Prayer is the most effective method in evangelism. Whether we call it just "prayer" or "prayer warfare" is not the issue; you need to pray. A prayerless Christian is a powerless one, so also a prayerful Christian is a powerful one. Through prayer, God will do great things. Make it your exercise to walk around your city or village and pray for the conversion of souls. Prayer is not only the key to revival, it is also the only key that unlocks the hearts of the unconverted. Without prayer, all methods of evangelism will fail.

Worship Evangelism.

When I was preaching in Australia last year, I was introduced to this method of evangelism when I saw groups of Christians go into the streets and sing. Just sing! They sang worship songs to the Lord; a bit like Christmas caroling. While one may not see immediate results through this method, it nonetheless gives the Christians boldness and the ability to work together as a team. It is a great witness to the community, and certainly gives glory to God.

New Methods.

As evangelists are innovators and great champions of change, they will not be restricted to one method, but will explore new ones. Today there are many powerful evangelism tools available. Look out for new methods. Do the undone. Make the impossible possible. Let the unheard of be heard. Jump into those opportunities!

Remember to avoid the temptation to do it your way instead of God's way. God's ways and methods are usually so different from our own as to be unimaginable. Biblically, some of God's ways for accomplishing great results have been perceived as strange or foolish: Hosea was ordered to do the appalling; John the Baptist was wild and weird in mannerism and method; God reduced Gideon's army to only three hundred to defeat an army of thousands; God commanded King Hezekiel and his host not to fight against the enemy, but to stand still; Samson used a jawbone to kill three thousand people.

A necessity for effectiveness is to realize our inability, inadequacy, and insignificance. God always uses weak instruments to do great things. We who want to evangelize must confess, like the Apostle Paul, "When I am weak, then I am strong" (II Corinthians 12:10).

Ultimately, the determining factor in evangelism is whether it brings honor and glory to God. That's what counts.

God is looking for people whom He will call and qualify. Go forth with joy!